PSYCHIC

PSYCHIC

My Life in Two Worlds

SYLVIA BROWNE

With Lindsay Harrison

HarperOne
An Imprint of HarperCollinsPublishers

HarperOne

HarperCollins books may be purchased for educational, business, or sales promotional use. For information, please write: Special Markets Department, HarperCollins Publishers, 10 East 53rd Street, New York, NY 10022.

HarperCollins Web site: http://www.harpercollins.com
HarperCollins®, ▥ ®, and HarperOne™ are
trademarks of HarperCollins Publishers

FIRST EDITION
Designed by Level C

Library of Congress Cataloging-in-Publication Data is available upon request.

ISBN 978–0–06–196672–9

10 11 12 13 14   RRD (H)   10 9 8 7 6 5 4 3 2 1

To every client, every audience member,
everyone who's ever read my books,
everyone who's ever touched my life along the way—
you've contributed more to this book
and to the journey of my soul
than I can ever repay.

CONTENTS

PREFACE

I n case you're wondering why I've chosen now to write my memoir, let me make something clear right up front: I'm not retiring, and I'm certainly not going Home yet. I've got far too much left to do.

The simple answer to "Why now?" is that I've decided I'm ready to talk about my life and my work in my own words. In fact, I may make a habit of doing this every seventy-three years whether I need to or not.

To some of you who've read my other books and/or come to my lectures, many of the stories in this book will be familiar. To all of you, I promise there are stories in this book you've never read or heard before, stories we can all laugh about and cry about and learn from together.

I've included overviews of many of my philosophies and psychic experiences in these memoirs, and if you find yourselves wanting to read more about any or all of them, know that I've written entire books about each and every one of them. I've even written entire books about the fact that there's a Father God and a Mother God, by the way. So please don't let it throw you that for the majority of this book I refer to God simply, with male pronouns. The alternative is to use the word They, or He/She, which is just plain annoying. Besides, I don't believe for a moment that They care what we call Him/Her, as long as we commit our lives to His/Her service. (See what I mean? In writing, as in life, get too bogged down with technicalities and you miss the whole point.)

For the most part, though, this book isn't about the spiritual psychic I am. It's about the woman I am, not remotely psychic about myself. When I look back on this particular incarnation, I'm as mystified as you might be at the choices in my life that actually seemed like a good idea at the time. If you'll forgive the cliché, this isn't the story of a victim; it's the story of a survivor, flaws, missteps, and all.

It's coming straight from my soul to yours, and I truly hope you enjoy it.

Sylvia

GROWING UP PSYCHIC

I believe that before we come here from the Other Side to start a new incarnation, we write very detailed charts for our lifetimes to help guarantee that we accomplish the goals we set for ourselves. We choose our parents, our siblings, our friends, our enemies, our spouses, our children, our careers, our assets, our challenges, our health issues, our best and worst qualities, the best and worst qualities in those who are closest to us, and certainly the timing of it all.

As I look back on this long, strange, complicated life I've lived, I just have one question about the chart I wrote:

What the hell was I thinking?

IT'S VALENTINE'S DAY 2009. I'm seventy-two years old. I'm blind in one eye, and I have a limp from an irreparable crack in my femur (a lasting token of my first husband's esteem). I'm standing at the head of an aisle in an ivory silk dress, holding a bouquet, surrounded by a room full of family, friends, and my Novus Spiritus ministers. Smiling confidently back at me from beneath the arch at the end of the aisle is a tall, handsome, sixty-two-year-old man named Michael Ulery. In the year we've been together he's seen me at my best and my worst, and he's been nothing but kind, supportive, patient, hard working, and thoughtful. He's so good natured and in such a perpetually good mood that I frequently stare at him, especially first thing in the morning when he brings me coffee without my asking, and say, "What's wrong with you?"

Michael is a successful jewelry designer and businessman. I first saw him in a jewelry store near my office in Campbell, California, at a time in my life when my position on relationships was a firm, nonnegotiable, "Spare me." So you could have knocked me over with a feather when I found myself asking the store owner about the attractive man behind the counter who was busy helping another customer. On our first date a week or so later he apologetically admitted that when we were introduced he didn't have the first clue who I was. Just when I thought he couldn't be more perfect. And the rest, as they say, is history.

So here I am, limping down the aisle into marriage number four (or number five, but only on a technicality), impossibly happy but also chagrined at the fact that obviously, when I was on the Other Side writing my chart, it seemed like a great idea to wait until I was in my seventies to meet the real Mr. Right. I repeat—what the hell was I thinking?

Then again, if it took this long, and this much, to get to this moment, I might write that same chart all over again.

————

TO GET THE requisite details out of the way: I was born Sylvia Celeste Shoemaker in Kansas City, Missouri, on October 19, 1936.

My father Bill and I adored each other from the moment we first laid eyes on each other. He was a good-looking, funny, warm, affectionate extrovert who made me feel like the most important person in the world when he'd wink at me and say, "That's my girl." He was a postman who exercised his love of show business by emceeing all sorts of local events, and even in the worst of times we could make each other laugh until we cried.

And then there was my mother. Celeste. As mean, self-involved, humorless, and disconnected a woman as you'd ever hope to meet. She was physically abusive when my father wasn't around, and she delighted in telling me about lying awake at night trying to figure out how she could kill me and get away with it. Her way of dealing with situations that displeased her was to retire to her bathtub and soak herself into pretending they didn't exist, which is probably why I remember her as being prune-y most of the time. My father had several affairs throughout his marriage to my mother, and I didn't blame him. In fact, I always believed that the only reason he never left her is that he would have had to kiss her good-bye.

I've come to know that there are people in this world called "dark entities." Dark entities are those who, because they've turned away from God and abandoned His light, choose to spread nothing but darkness in their lives. By their own choice, when they die, their spirits don't transcend to the sacred perfection of the Other Side. Instead, they enter what's known as the Left Door, plunge through a Godless, joyless abyss, and cycle right back into some poor unsuspecting fetus again. If one of these days you read about someone in their late teens triggering a violent uprising in some historically peaceful country, you can confidently say to yourself, "Oh, look, it's Sylvia's mother."

It seems important to add that I took care of my mother in the last years of her life. My Gnostic Christian beliefs demanded nothing less, and beliefs without the actions to back them up are nothing but rhetoric. I admit it: I did it more for my own peace of mind and my certainty that it was just plain the right thing to do than out of any delusion that she would have done the same for me.

My very earliest childhood memories involve my enraged mother chasing me through the hallway waving a wire hanger she intended to beat me with (after seeing the movie *Mommie Dearest* I wondered if my mother might have been the technical consultant); standing in my crib peering out the window, watching anxiously for Daddy's black car to pull into the driveway so I'd be safe from her for awhile; and the incident I've come to think of as The Time She Tried to Burn My Foot Off.

I was three years old. It was bath time. What I distinctly remember is Mother putting me into the tub, turning on a full blast of scalding hot water and leaving the room. My foot had to be treated for second-degree burns. Much of the aftermath is a little hazy. There was something about Mother explaining to Daddy that she'd had to leave me alone to answer the phone (take it from me, there was no phone call) and that she'd warned that damned building maintenance man a thousand times to stop cranking up the temperature of the water heater. And there was a loud conversation behind the closed door of my mother's bedroom between her and an aunt and uncle who threatened to take me to live with them if there was ever another hint of abuse, no matter how "accidental" she claimed it was.

That threat made Mother much more circumspect about hurting me—it never occurred to her to stop, but from then on she saw to it that there were never potential witnesses or visible marks. Not for a moment did her occasional, unpredictable bursts of rage inspire me to be more well behaved. They just inspired me to be faster, smarter, and angrier at her, until finally, when I was about seven, I ratted her out to Daddy. I can still hear his voice, and feel my heart bursting with love and gratitude for my brave, strong hero, as he turned to her and promised with quiet fury, "I've never raised my hand to a woman in my life, but if you ever touch that child in anger again, I will tear you apart."

I believed him. Clearly, so did she. She never physically hurt me again. Emotionally? Keep reading.

DISPELLING MUCH OF my mother's darkness throughout my childhood was the warm, loving flame of her mother, my grandmother Ada Coil. She was my inspiration, my mentor, my fearless defender, and the quiet sanctuary where my lifelong devotion to God had its roots. Without Grandma Ada, my life would have made no sense to me at all.

Grandma Ada was brilliantly psychic, another link in a three-hundred-year psychic family legacy. I was the next link in that legacy, complete with a caul, or fetal membrane, wrapped around my head at birth, thought to be the sign of a child born with "the gift." Grandma Ada didn't tell me about the caul or its significance for several years, to avoid programming me for expectations that might never manifest. Instead she just watched and waited, loving me unconditionally, confident that if I really had inherited her psychic gift, there would be no stopping it, and no stopping me from expressing it.

She was right.

I HAVE NO memory of two psychic incidents that happened when I was three years old. But I'm told I informed my parents that I would have a baby sister when I was six (my only sibling, Sharon, was born a month before my sixth birthday). And I announced, "Grandpa's dead," moments before Daddy arrived home one sad afternoon to break the news that his father had just passed away from a sudden heart attack.

Instead, my memory flashes from those days are limited to things that really mattered, like riding my beloved tricycle and being enchanted by fireflies and learning that roller skates worked much better on the sidewalk than they did on our grassy front yard. Doing my dolls' hair, or hostessing tea parties for my stuffed animals?

When I could be outside playing "ditch 'em" with the other kids in the neighborhood? Not a chance, thanks. (In case you're not familiar with ditch 'em, just think hide and seek after dark with flashlights.)

In fact, with the exception of Mother's intermittent volatility, my early childhood was so ordinary that it made my first genuine psychic experience feel like a horrible ambush. I was five years old, pushing vegetables around on my plate at a boring Sunday family dinner, when I happened to glance over at my great-grandmother Hattie Braun. In less than a second her face went from perfectly normal to hideous, melting like hot wax down onto her neck, exposing her skull, nothing but gaping cavities where her eyes, nose, and mouth used to be. I froze, terrified, while she and everyone else at the table went right on idly eating and chatting away as if nothing unusual was happening. Finally I managed to tear my focus away from her and turned for comfort to my other great-grandmother Sarah Shoemaker, who was sitting next to me, which drove me to sheer panic when I saw that her face was melting too, just like Hattie's.

I leapt up from the table and ran to my father, grabbing his arm and begging him to take me home. I was hysterical, and I'm sure everyone was both worried and relieved when he made a quick, apologetic exit, carried me outside, and asked me what was wrong. Needless to say, it was no help when all I could do was repeat over and over again through my tears, "Their faces were melting! Their faces were melting!"

Great-Grandmother Hattie and Great-Grandmother Sarah passed away within the next two weeks, just four days apart, and with a typical child's logic of believing that everything that goes wrong is her fault, I was sure that somehow, thanks to those grotesque visions, I'd killed them. Shaken by the trauma, the isolation of my parents' inability to understand what I was talking about, and the guilt of thinking I'd personally ended two sweet, harmless lives, I became a depressed, withdrawn, deeply troubled little girl.

For the first of more times than I can count, Grandma Ada reached her strong hand into my confusion and pulled me out. She arrived at our house one day not long after my great-grandmothers' deaths, recognized that something was very wrong with her cherished granddaughter, gently took me into her lap and said, "Whatever it is, you can tell me, my sweetheart."

I burst into tears and sobbed my way through the story of the melting faces no one else saw and the two resulting murders I'd clearly committed. Instead of staring at me as if I'd just grown antennae, she held me closer and said, "First of all, I promise, you didn't do one thing to Hattie and Sarah. They just finished their time here, and their bodies were old and tired, so they asked God to bring them Home. They're happy and healthy now, living in heaven with Jesus and the saints and all the Angels, and it didn't have a single thing to do with you."

It made me feel a little better, and I asked if she was sure. She nodded and wiped away my tears before she added, "Second of all, I'm sorry for what you saw that night at dinner. It must have been very scary."

"You mean, you believe me, Grandma?"

"Of course I believe you," she assured me. "I know exactly what it's like to see things that other people don't see, and I know exactly how alone it can make you feel. But it's nothing to be frightened about, sweetheart; it's because God gave us a gift that we'll have with us all our lives. You and I are something called 'psychic.'"

A gift? Was she kidding? "No! I don't want to be psychic!" I protested through a new wave of tears. "It's ugly, and I hate it, and I don't want to see melting faces for the rest of my life!"

"Then here's what we'll do," she said. "We'll just ask God to never show you anything ever again that's too scary or upsetting for you to handle."

Before I could argue, she closed her eyes and began to pray. I prayed with her, and kept right on praying, and while I could fill libraries with books on the psychic visions I've had since then, I've never been given another one that was more emotionally challenging than I could take.

Looking back, it's extraordinary how significant that afternoon was in the course of my life. It gave me a very special connection to a woman I deeply loved, trusted, and admired. It gave me permission to embrace rather than apologize for what had happened to me because it came from God. It gave me a word—*psychic*—to call what had happened, which made it seem a little safer and less freakish. And although I wasn't sure I understood or even quite believed this part yet, Grandma Ada, who never lied to me, said it was a gift, so I could at least try to figure out what it was.

Almost immediately I began noticing that every night after I turned off my nightstand lamp, my bedroom began filling with spirits. None of them seemed interested in me; they just milled around among themselves like opaque shadows. To this day I'm not sure if I was becoming more finely tuned to the higher frequency of the Other Side or if my reluctant acceptance of being psychic attracted them to someone they knew would be able to see them, in a kind of "Party in Sylvia's room!" celebration. What I am sure of is that while I never believed they meant me any harm, I found it unnerving to try to go to sleep with a semi-transparent crowd floating around the bed.

I mentioned it to my mother, who immediately began drawing a hot bath for herself. I mentioned it to my father, who had long since become accustomed to having a psychic mother-in-law but didn't have a clue what to say or do about it.

I mentioned it to Grandma Ada, who'd had the same problem since she was a child, and she calmly handed me a flashlight to take to bed with me. (I still can't sleep in a completely dark room, by the way. And if your children tell you they're upset by spirits visiting them during the night, don't tell them they're imagining things.

They're not. Just assure them the spirits would never hurt them and give them a flashlight.)

Before long spirits began appearing any time, anywhere, and one incident taught me two interesting lessons: that visions differ from one psychic to the next, and that psychics aren't psychic about themselves. (For more proof of that second lesson, read the rest of this book.) One day Grandma Ada and I were tearing the house apart looking for a steel strongbox that contained some papers she urgently needed. When we got around to her bedroom, I saw Great Grandmother Hattie, Ada's deceased mother, materialize and point to the back of a massive dresser. I shared this news with Grandma Ada, who hadn't seen a thing, and it triggered her memory of hiding the strongbox behind the dresser where no one (including her, obviously) would ever think to look for it.

A few nights later the family was gathered in the living room when I saw a spirit take shape behind Grandma Ada's left shoulder. "Grandma," I asked, "who is that man behind you?"

Daddy, too accustomed to this kind of thing to even glance in our direction, went right on reading. Mother rolled her eyes and made a break for the nearest bathtub. Grandma Ada asked me what he looked like.

I described him as tall, with reddish-colored hair and round wire-rimmed glasses, and I added, "There's a string around his neck, and it has a horn on it that he uses to listen to people's chests."

"It's my Uncle Jim!" she gasped, more thrilled than I'd ever seen her. He'd been her favorite uncle, a doctor who'd died twenty-four years earlier in a flu epidemic, and she gave me an ecstatic hug to thank me for letting her know that this man she'd missed so much was around her.

So there really was an up side to this psychic thing. Who knew?

———

FROM THAT NIGHT on, it was as if floodgates had opened. I routinely saw spirits around almost everyone. I knew who was calling or coming to visit before the phone or doorbell rang. I guilelessly asked Daddy, in front of my mother, who the nice blonde lady was he was going to visit when he made some excuse to leave the house for the evening. I warned even the most casual passersby that there was something wrong with their liver or their gall bladder or their spleen before I even knew what livers, gall bladders, and spleens were. I can only imagine how relieved my family was when the time came for me to start school.

My Jewish father, my Episcopalian mother, and my Lutheran grandmother were united in their belief that I was in serious need of some structure, strong guidance, and constructive focus. They weren't wrong. I hadn't learned yet how to control the images that surrounded me or how to separate myself from the psychic impact of the emotional and physical force fields everyone unconsciously gives off. I could easily become exhausted, depressed, anxious, or even physically ill in large groups of people from sheer extrasensory overload, depending on the moods and/or health problems of anyone in my involuntary radar. I still loved being with my neighborhood playmates, but I was beginning to feel isolated since none of them seemed to see what I saw, sense what I sensed, or know what I knew. From what I'd heard about school, there would be new things to learn and be stimulated by and a whole new group of children to make friends with, and I couldn't wait.

Somehow the Lutheran in the family came up with the idea that the perfect answer to my need for structure, guidance, and grounding would be a convent. Even more remarkably, the Jew and the Episcopalian agreed with her. In what seemed like the blink of an eye, Grandma Ada, Daddy, Mother, and I were all taking instruction in Catholicism and being baptized together in the church, and my formal education was placed in the firm, steady hands of nuns.

I loved school. I loved learning. I loved being surrounded by friends my own age who playfully lured me outside of my own head for hours at a time. And I especially loved the nuns. I was in awe of their dedication and commitment and the fact that they knew God and Jesus and the Angels personally. I began wearing black around the house with a white hand towel draped across my chest, an improvised homage to the nuns' habits, and I announced to anyone who'd listen that I was going to be a nun when I grew up. (Pause for exhales of relief from Catholics around the world that I clearly changed my mind.)

My sister Sharon came along shortly after I started school. She was born without a caul and without an apparent psychic bone in her body, although I'll always believe that everyone has psychic abilities, whether they put them to active use or not. In other words, from the beginning Sharon was something I yearned to be but couldn't accomplish for the life of me: she was "normal" without just pretending to be. According to our mother, that wasn't the only difference between us. She must have said a thousand times, to us and to everyone else, "Sharon's the pretty one, and Sylvia's the one with the personality." On the slim chance that she intended it as a compliment, neither of us ever heard it that way. Instead what we heard was, "Sylvia's ugly, and Sharon has the personality of a flounder." I'm sure the carefully cultivated sibling rivalry between us, along with our six-year age difference and the fact that we were simply two very different people kept us from ever being best friends, but we were closely involved in each other's lives.

And there's no doubt that I was psychically tuned in to her. Daddy and I had begun the tradition of spending Saturdays together, just the two of us, doing some kind of activity—roller skating at the local rink, fishing, paddle boating, or our favorite pastime, going to movies, usually preceded by an hour at the newsstand browsing through *Photoplay* and every other movie magazine we loved. One day, during a matinee of *Stage Door Canteen*, which we were thoroughly enjoying, I found myself feeling dizzy and gasping for air. I panicked, wondering if maybe I was dying, until I realized that I was fine; it was my baby sister who was in trouble. I grabbed Daddy's arm and began frantically pulling him out of his seat toward the exit. He understandably resisted until I screamed, "It's Sharon! She can't breathe! We have to go right now!" He was at a dead run right behind me by the time we reached our car, and as we pulled into our driveway my mother raced out of the house sobbing that Sharon couldn't breathe and was turning blue and our phone wasn't working. Daddy sped off to the hospital with Sharon, who had contracted double pneumonia and arrived at the emergency room with only minutes to spare.

In other words, I was still "knowing" things without a clue how I knew them and still seeing spirits day and night. But school, friends, the wise, all-knowing nuns, and endless worlds to explore thanks to my newly acquired skills of reading and writing (don't get me started on 'rithmetic) were making me feel more balanced and more grounded. I found myself wondering if maybe, at the risk of sounding like an ingrate, this "gift" from God would gradually fade away and I could finally just be a little girl who'd ask, "Did you see that?" and everyone around me would say, "Yes."

ANY HOPE OF the gift fading away vanished one night when I was eight years old, a night that would dramatically affect the rest of my life. I was in bed, under strict orders to go straight to sleep, so of course I was playing with my flashlight, beaming it around the room as the usual opaque shadows of spirits silently gathered to mingle. With no warning, the beam of light began to grow and intensify into an almost blinding white-gold glow, and while I gaped at it in awe a woman's voice resonated from deep inside it, in a rapid, unearthly chirp. "Don't be afraid, Sylvia," the voice said. "I come from God."

At that moment I didn't care if the voice came from God or Albuquerque, I was out of there, flying out the door in absolute terror and racing down the stairs to the kitchen, where Grandma Ada was cleaning vegetables from her Victory Garden. I slammed into her and held on for dear life, sobbing through the story of what had just happened.

"That was your Spirit Guide, dear," she explained calmly, stroking my hair. "Pick up the carrots."

A Spirit Guide, it turns out, is someone who, when we decide to come to earth for another incarnation, agrees to be our vigilant companion and helpmate while we're away from Home. They've studied our charts and know what we intend to accomplish here, and it's their assignment to encourage, support, and advise us along the way without interfering with our charts or depriving us of our free will.

As I've learned over all these decades, their messages to us are so typically subtle, and spoken so directly to our subconscious minds where our spirits live, that it's easy to mistake them for our own instincts, or a "sudden impulse" or the ever-popular "Something told me to. . . ." An instinct prompts us to change dinner reservations at the last minute from one restaurant to another, and we run into someone at that second restaurant whom we needed to see, whether the reason we needed to see them is immediately apparent or not. We take a different route than usual when heading to work one morning on a "sudden impulse" and discover later that, by doing so, we avoided an accident. "Something tells us to" call a friend we haven't talked to in awhile and, it turns out, she has the solution to a problem we've been worried about or helpful information we didn't even anticipate needing. In fact, as a good rule of thumb, every time you write off an impulse with the words "Something told me to . . ." change that to "Some*one* told me to . . ." and chances are you'll be much more accurate. A Spirit Guide isn't Batman or Wonder Woman. Our Guides aren't with us to ride to our rescue whenever we're in trouble. They're with us to support us through the trouble we charted for ourselves and gently see to it that, according to our own plans for this lifetime, we're where we're supposed to be when we're supposed to be there, doing what we need to do, for better or worse, to study the lessons we've chosen to come here to learn.

Grandma Ada seemed impressed that in addition to being clairvoyant, or able to see beings and objects that originate in another dimension, I had now become clairaudient, or able to hear them, as well. I loved impressing her and tried to smile, but privately I was thinking, "Just shoot me."

Not for the first or last time, I couldn't have been more wrong. My Spirit Guide's voice has been a constant, invaluable presence in my life, and in the lives of others, since the night she introduced herself in my bedroom. She lived her one incarnation on earth as an Aztec-Incan who, at the age of nineteen, was killed by a spear in 1520 while protecting her infant daughter during the Spanish invasion of Colombia. She told me her name was Ilena. I apparently either didn't care for that or couldn't remember it, because I promptly renamed her Francine and have never called her anything else. She's never objected, which is a good lesson for all of you who have no idea what your Spirit Guide's name might be: they couldn't be less concerned with what we call them, they're only concerned *that* we call them.

———————

FOR THE RECORD, by the way, I didn't actually see Francine that first night. While many others have seen her over all these decades, I only had one quick glimpse of her, during a meltdown in my late teens, and I deliberately looked away before she'd fully materialized. But that's another story for later in this chapter.

Communicating with Francine became a daily routine, although it took me awhile to get accustomed to her voice. Like every other spirit I've talked to, she lives on the Other Side, our real Home, from where we all came and to where we'll all return, which exists on a much higher frequency than ours on earth. The result is that spirit voices sound very much like a tape played on fast forward or, for those of you who are old enough to remember, Alvin of Chipmunk fame. I learned quickly to understand her, though, and to appreciate her as yet another fascinating source of new information, no less interesting than school continued to be.

So imagine my delight one day in class when one of the nuns decided to teach us that while our bodies inevitably die, our spirits survive death. Eager to validate this reassuring bit of news, I chimed in that I happened to know that was true, because I saw and talked to spirits all the time.

Now, imagine my utter shock when I found myself on the receiving end of a tirade from an enraged nun. She was appalled that I would commit such heresy in her classroom by making up such an outrageous lie, and I'd be staying after school to give me a little extra time to get my fresh mouth under control.

I didn't understand it then, and I don't understand it now: it makes sense to almost every religion on earth that our spirits survive death, but it's sacrilege to believe we can communicate with them? What possible sense does *that* make? And how could it possibly be sacrilege, when I knew I loved God every bit as much as any nun in that convent? Maybe even more to the point, accusing me of making up a reality I'd been living since I was four years old confused me as much as if I'd been accused of making up my parents.

I was beside myself when I got home from school that day. But not nearly as beside myself as Grandma Ada was when I explained to her why I was so late. After assuring me that I'd done nothing wrong, she grabbed her handbag and marched off to school, where she and the nun had "a talk." That's all she told me, but I would love to have been a fly on the wall—that nun never again accused me of making things up or punished me for sincerely trying to contribute to a discussion. Of course, I was also thought of as a bit of a troublemaker from then on, but because the faculty knew I genuinely admired them and meant no disrespect when I did speak up, we got along beautifully for the most part.

I GOT AN extraordinary education over the next several years, although some of it continued to confuse me. From what the Catholics told me, we are all created by an all-knowing, all-loving, perfect God who adores us unconditionally—unless we commit mortal sins like not going to confession, not being Catholic, getting divorced, using birth control, or eating meat on Fridays, in which case He'll smite us and send us to burn in the fires of hell for the rest of all eternity. (Huh? And by the way, in recent years the church has decided that it's okay for the Catholics to eat meat on Fridays after all. So what happens to those poor people who were sent to hell for that? Do they get transferred to heaven now, or what?) If we obeyed all His rules, we would go to heaven when we died, and then . . . uh. . . . (They were a little hazy about what heaven looks like or what we do with ourselves when we get there.) God promised us eternal lives, but these lives we're living now are the first ones we've ever had. (So where have we been for all these eons since time began?)

And then there was confession, which completely mystified me. I went to my first confession when I was eleven, and because even at that age I was a chronic overachiever, I had my heart set on being thorough and well prepared to impress the priest with what a devout little Catholic I was. Days ahead of time I began writing down all the sins I wanted to confess to: talking back to my mother, telling my sister she had cooties even though she probably didn't (I was never quite sure what cooties were, I just knew Sharon didn't seem to want them), telling my parents I brushed my teeth twice one day when I only brushed them once. . . . It seemed like a pretty lame list for my first confession, so I made up a few other infractions of equal gravity, reverently took my seat in the confessional, and began in a trembling little voice, "Forgive me, Father, for I have sinned."

I was only on about my third "sin" when the priest heard me shuffling my paperwork and asked what I was doing. Rather than praising me for my diligence in preparing a list, he gave me a very indignant scolding. What if I'd misplaced my list and someone had come across it, he demanded? How could I be so careless and risk exposure like that? Imagine the shame if it found its way into the wrong hands?

Granted, I was only eleven. But I was old enough to know an over-reaction when I heard one. Shame? Was he kidding? I didn't murder someone, I wasn't running a prostitution ring in my neighborhood. I just mouthed off to my sister and mother and exaggerated my dental hygiene duties for one big-deal day. At worst, I wasn't planning to do any bragging about that behavior. "Shame" never entered my mind. I managed to accept my assignment of a thousand Hail Marys or whatever it was without giving the priest a piece of my mind, but I also started wondering about the whole ritual of confession. If God loves each of us equally, as we were being taught in Catholic school, why did I need this stern, disapproving priest to atone on my behalf? Why couldn't I just ask Him for forgiveness myself? What was the message here—that I wasn't worthy to talk to God without an in-termediary? And if that was the case, then why had I been taught to pray directly to Him with devout regularity for as long as I could remember?

In the meantime, while I was becoming more confused than com-forted by the rules and dogma of the church, Francine was chirping away about the Other Side where she lived and where the vast ma-

jority of us live—yes, even the non-Catholics—when we're not slogging along here on earth by our own choice for the spiritual growth
of our souls. The Other Side, she told me, is a very real place, our
real Home, just three feet above and identical to the earth's surface,
existing at a much higher frequency so that we don't perceive its immediate proximity. We lead busy, active, blissful lives there among
the messiahs, the Angels, our loved ones from every life we've ever
lived on earth and at Home, and the palpable presence of God Himself. As for hell, there is no such thing, nor is there any such thing as
a God so petty and vengeful that He would subject a beloved child
to eternal punishment because they violated some human-made rule.
God doesn't turn His back on anyone, but there are those who turn
away from Him, and they face their own self-inflicted punishment
by recycling over and over again through the Left Door and back to
earth for another incarnation, denying themselves the joyful peace
that's waiting for them on the Other Side.

———————

I TOOK IN all this information from the church and from Francine
like the good, perpetually curious student I was. I knew which point
of view made more sense to me, but beyond an absolute belief in
God and Jesus, I had a lot of studying to do and questions to ask
before I was ready to commit to exactly what I did and didn't believe. And frankly, I was too busy being a psychic but otherwise
normal teenager, overachieving my way through school and dealing
with family drama to give it much thought.

When I was sixteen, the chaotic rage between my parents and the
new woman in my father's life made it look as if my parents' marriage
was finally going to end. I might have been their most enthusiastic
supporter if the indecision and guilt hadn't been so horribly painful
for Daddy, and if a hideous custody battle hadn't been so inevitable.
Sharon, "the pretty one," had grown into an introverted, insecure

girl who was joined at the hip with our mother, so there was no question where she would go. She and I exemplified the interesting phenomenon of two siblings with the same parents and the same upbringing being polar opposites in so many ways, and Sharon was the poster child for how damaging it is to attach yourself to a dark entity. While I kept my distance from our mother and basked in the bright, positive sunshine of a father who believed there was nothing I couldn't do, Sharon clung to a woman who virtually crippled her with negative reinforcement. "Sharon can't do that," Mother would say, referring to anything from simple chores to playing. "You know how frail/fragile/delicate she is." And of course Sharon believed her and became as frail/fragile/delicate as she'd been programmed to be. Daddy and I would go laughing and stampeding down the stairs and out the door for one adventure after another, leaving Mother and Sharon in our wake, each in their separate, darkened bedrooms, Mother in her perpetual leopard print robe, somehow gratified that she'd finally been able to snare a willing, dependent hostage in this bizarre collection of people we called a family.

For obvious reasons, given a choice if and when my parents separated, I would have walked out the door with Daddy in a heartbeat, but he was in no emotional shape to offer me a stable home as a single parent. I would have ended up living with Mother and Sharon and without Daddy, which sounded like no life at all to me. To complete the feeling that the earth was crumbling away beneath my feet, Grandma Ada's health seemed to be failing, and Francine had no better advice to offer about any of this than "It will all work out exactly as it's meant to." That happens to be true, but do you find it helpful when someone says it to you? Me neither. And when I was sixteen, it absolutely infuriated me.

Then, with all the foresight and maturity of a teenager, I came up with the perfect solution: I'd get married! Yeah! That should work! Then I wouldn't have to worry about which of my parents I was going to live with—I'd live with my husband and start a life and a family of my own, and it wouldn't matter any more whether or not Daddy and Mother stayed together.

I was dating a couple of boys at the time. Joe and Warren. I decided that Joe was the likelier of the two to leap in to help me with this terrible dilemma I was in, and he'd already said that he wanted to marry me someday. He didn't specify what he meant by "someday," but under the circumstances, why couldn't it mean, oh, let's say, tomorrow?

Sure enough, Joe, having exactly as much foresight and maturity as I did, thought it was a great idea. That night, after a brilliant performance of nonchalance at the family dinner table, I managed to find my birth certificate and transformed myself from a sixteen-year-old to an eighteen-year-old with a quick, artistic stroke of a pen.

After school the next day Joe and I jumped on a streetcar, went across the state line to Kansas City, Kansas, and promised in front of a justice of the peace to love, honor, and obey each other 'til death did us part, or whatever it was we repeated on cue for the five or ten minutes it took. Who listened? We were sixteen, and I'm sure the reality and stark "officialness" of what we were doing terrified Joe as much as it did me once the no-frills, sterile, assembly-line ceremony got under way. (In case you're wondering, by the way, the bride was resplendent in a white pinafore with oh-so-fashionable white bobby sox and Oxfords.)

On the streetcar back to Kansas City, Missouri, we briefly discussed the possibility of a honeymoon. It was Friday, and we had a whole weekend ahead of us before school on Monday morning. The fact that neither of us had any money was trivial compared to the far bigger drawback: we weren't planning to tell our parents about this until the time was right, whatever that meant, so the chances of their approving of a two-day honeymoon weren't good. We ended up heading off to our respective homes an hour past curfew.

Mother was in the living room, glaring angrily at the clock, when I came tiptoeing in. "Where have you been, young lady?" she demanded. "And what's that under your dress?"

I looked down at myself and saw a painfully obvious lump in my bridal pinafore. I tried, too late, to flatten it and finally, lamely answered, "Nothing. Just a, uh, license."

"A license? For what? What kind of license?" She was yelling now, and I went flying up the stairs to my room, sobbing my eyes out by the time I slammed the door, horrified and remorseful and wishing to God the last few hours had never happened.

Mother sprinted to the bathtub while Daddy took over. He pounded at my door, demanding that I let him in. As he and the pounding grew louder and louder, my anxiety and remorse grew worse and worse, until they spilled over into enough desperation to explode, "You can't come in! I'm a married woman now!"

Not for long. I'll spare you the humiliating details, but Daddy may have set a record for the quickest annulment in the history of nuptial bliss, and Joe and I were forbidden by our parents from ever seeing each other again outside of school. Although he and I never talked about it, I know Joe had to be as relieved as I was.

All without missing a single day of school.

––––––––

OF COURSE, NOTHING had changed in the impending separation and custody issues between my parents, and while I deeply appreciated being single again, I was even more lost than before and even more eager to bury myself in my friends, activities, and school, where things at least seemed to make sense.

It had become a source of fascination to me, as it still is today, that the more you learn, the more there is to learn. In fact, I'd become so enthralled with my studies that I abandoned the idea of becoming a nun and decided Grandma Ada was right: I was meant to be a teacher. I loved everything about English, creative writing, and poetry. I loved typing and shorthand. I loved almost everything about home ec—I excelled at cooking and needlepoint, but sewing and I held each other in mutual contempt from the moment we met.

I took tap and ballet lessons, the "lesson" in this case being that I should never be allowed anywhere near tap or ballet shoes again in this lifetime. In sharp contrast, Daddy and I began taking ballroom dance lessons as one of our traditional Saturday activities, entered a few local contests and won them, mind you, which more than made up for my lack of a future as the lead Sugar Plum Fairy in *The Nutcracker*.

I developed my first real crush. His name was Mario Lanza, and he starred in a movie called *The Great Caruso*, which I must have seen a million times (or, okay, maybe twelve). I bought all his records and sang along with them at the top of my lungs in perfect phonetic Italian until everyone within earshot begged me to stop. Sadly, my passion was unrequited. I blame the fact that we never actually met.

And I was blessed with lots of friends, partly because I was an extrovert and made a point of being a good friend myself, and partly because, as my friend Mary Margaret had put it since kindergarten, when I accurately told her that her mother's arm would be broken and her father would lose his job, I "knew things." I don't think a week went by without a classmate or even one of the nuns pulling me aside to ask for some kind of psychic insight. Mary Margaret came to believe that I could be lying under a bus, bloody and barely breathing, and as my friends pulled me to safety they'd be pelting me with questions in case I didn't make it—"Is my boyfriend cheating on me?" and "Is Bobby going to invite me to the prom?" and "Am I going to pass my chemistry final next week?"

Two incidents in particular are as clear in my memory as if they happened earlier this week. In one I "saw" my friend Joan fracturing her skull on the dashboard of a blue car, and I begged her to stay out of blue cars for awhile. Before long she was heading off to run errands with a family friend and she saw that her friend was driving a blue car. She remembered my warning and stayed home. A few hours later the blue car's brakes failed and it was wrapped around a telephone pole, the passenger side where Joan would have been sitting completely destroyed.

The other started innocently enough. My friend Linda stopped by to show off the crepe paper witch costume she planned to wear to a Halloween party that night, and the moment I opened the door I "saw" her and her costume engulfed in flames. I didn't say a word—"Don't let it catch fire" seemed like a pretty lame piece of advice—so I just made an appropriate fuss over how fabulous it was and laughed with her as she leapt and spun around the room practicing menacing witch behavior. But within minutes she whirled too close to the heating grate, and her skirt ignited. I don't doubt for a moment that "seeing" it before it happened allowed me to help rather than panic, because I'd thrown her to the floor and rolled her up in an area rug before she even realized she was smoldering. She left the house shaken but unharmed and headed off to shop for a new less flammable costume.

———

AFTER SEVERAL MONTHS of nasty, chaotic uncertainty, my parents reconciled. I was never quite sure how or why, or how much my desperate two-hour marriage stunt had to do with it, and I never asked. I was sure it didn't involve candlelit dinners and violinists playing "Fascination" while Mother and Daddy gazed into each other's eyes with renewed longing, so I settled for the sheer relief that it didn't look as if there were going to be any logistical changes in my immediate future. We still bore no resemblance to the *Leave It to Beaver* Cleaver family, but there was less fear, rage, and depression in the air now that words like *divorce, alimony,* and *custody* had been removed from the equation.

To the best of my knowledge, that near-divorce convinced Daddy once and for all that dating while married was ultimately more trouble than it was worth. A lot of men would have caught on much sooner. But a lot of men weren't married to Celeste.

I think I was about ten years old when I came home from school one day to find a big black sedan pulling away from the curb and Daddy, alone in the house, struggling to his feet just inside the front door, holding his bloody head that looked (probably accurately) as if it had come in violent contact with a heavy blunt instrument. He refused to tell me what had happened, or to call the police or his doctor, he simply kept assuring me that he was fine and it was nothing for me to worry about. But not long after that I was playing in the front yard when that same black sedan came speeding around the corner and screeched to a stop a few feet away from me.

The driver, a hulking man with mean dark eyes, rolled down his window and gave me a message to pass along to Daddy: "Tell him I'm coming to get you if he doesn't stay away from my wife."

I dutifully, and fearfully, delivered the message. Judging by Daddy's reaction, being bashed in the head with a baseball bat was a trip to Disneyland compared to even a hint of some harm coming to me, and that was the end of whatever had gone on between him and Mrs. Black Sedan.

Now, several years and girlfriends later, he'd faced the prospect of losing me again, along with Sharon and everyone and everything else he loved, and he'd decided it wasn't worth it. If my mother happened to be part of that package, then, oh well, it was, all things considered, a small price to pay.

Such as it was, my family was intact again, and I felt as if I'd climbed back onto slightly more solid ground again.

Then the sky fell in.

———

I WAS EIGHTEEN and a freshman at St. Theresa's College in Kansas City, majoring in education and literature with a minor in theology. I was exhilarated, inspired, and ready to conquer the world. The call from Daddy one deceptively normal morning telling me that Grandma Ada had been rushed to the hospital sent me into that numb, ear-ringing shock you never forget or quite recover from. She'd been diagnosed with a heart condition a few months earlier and had been warned that it was very serious, but through the magic of denial I'd convinced myself that the doctors were wrong and she'd be fine—this was my Grandma Ada, for God's sake. Nothing was going to happen to her. She was indestructible. Besides, there was no one on earth I loved as much, no one I relied on or trusted more, no one I needed more to keep me grounded and hopeful and unafraid. I'd never spent a day of my life without her, and I couldn't possibly start now, when everything around me was so new and unfamiliar.

She was in an oxygen tent, her eyes closed, when I walked into her room. Her face was utterly peaceful. Not a trace of pain or fear. I knew in the first instant of looking at her that she was joyfully going Home. I could barely breathe as I moved to her bed and selfishly whispered, "Please don't go, Grandma. I love you so much." She opened her eyes, just for a moment, and while she was much too weak to say a word, I heard her voice, strong and clear, promise, "I'll send you a sign when I get there."

I didn't leave the hospital for the next three days while Mother, Daddy, and Sharon came and went, and I was alone with her when her body quietly gave out. I was sure my heart would break. It was insane to me that the rest of the world seemed to go right on with its trivial busy-ness as if it didn't know or care that it had just been diminished.

Francine chirped away to assure me that Grandma Ada had reached the Other Side in no time and enjoyed an ecstatic reunion with countless loved ones who were waiting at the entrance to greet her. It was the first time I realized how selfish grief really is. I couldn't separate from my own loss enough to be happy for her. And yes, I could see and hear the spirit world, but there was no way that seeing or hearing her could possibly take the place of her tangible presence. I hope I didn't tell Francine to shut up, but I can honestly say I might have.

My boyfriend at the time, another Joe, picked me up first thing the next morning to take me for a quiet ride and help me escape the family gathering to plan the funeral. We drove in silence for mile after mile, going nowhere except away, both of us sadly aware that no matter how far we went, we couldn't create enough distance between me and my pain to make a difference.

I barely heard him when, after an hour or so, he quietly said, "Uh . . . Sylvia . . . ?"

I glanced at him and saw that he was looking at something in his rearview mirror. "I don't want to frighten you, but . . . your grandmother's in the back seat."

I couldn't bring myself to turn around. Instead, I stared straight ahead, and, very gradually, I began to sense her presence and detect the faint fragrance of her favorite lavender scent. Then I slowly let my eyes wander to the rearview mirror, and I gasped at the sight of Grandma Ada, in her favorite blue dress, peaceful, beaming with perfect health, eyes sparkling, smiling that smile of hers. I quickly turned to reach for her, but in the instant it took, she disappeared.

I know what you're thinking. Despite the fact that I'd been seeing spirits for as long as I could remember, I clearly missed her and needed her so much that I just had one of those grief-induced hallucinations "experts" talk about at times like these.

What made no sense to me then, and what makes no sense to me now: if that was a grief-induced hallucination, why was it Joe, who barely knew her and at most was simply sad for me, who saw her first? And since he described her perfectly with no prompting from me when we talked about it later, we can also eliminate the possibility that he was only trying to comfort me by claiming to see her in the back seat of his car.

Call it a hunch, but there are times when I have a feeling the experts don't know what they're talking about.

———

THERE WAS ANOTHER aspect to Grandma Ada's death that made it even more tragic. All her life she had deeply loved and taken care of her son, my uncle, whom we all called "Brother." He was born with a birth defect that left him terribly crippled, an invalid with any number of challenges. Don't ever let anyone convince you that the physically or mentally debilitated are being punished for some horrible past-life sin. Those who chart lives for themselves in which they face struggles many of us can only sympathize with are highly advanced spirits, and Brother was no exception. He was as sweet, dear, and brave a soul as I've ever met. In fact, when I was a child he almost lost his life saving mine.

I was playing in the front yard, completely absorbed in whatever shiny object had captured my attention, when I suddenly heard Brother's voice yelling, "Run! Run!" from inside the house. I looked toward his voice and saw him struggling out the door toward me as fast as his body would allow, terrified and focused on something behind me. I turned around to face a huge, wild-eyed woman, her skin ghostly white, her hair flying, her fists clenched and waving around in a rage as she headed straight at me.

Brother screamed, "Run, Sylvia!" again and managed to move himself between me and this oncoming madwoman, shielding me from her with his small, frail body and taking the full force of an assault that had been intended for me. The woman easily knocked him down and began violently beating him while I screamed at the top of my lungs and tried to pull her away from him. Grandma Ada and two neighbors heard my screams and raced to Brother's rescue. It took all of them to grab the woman and subdue her until the police arrived. She turned out to be the schizophrenic daughter of another neighbor and she lived at home under the dubious care of a full-time psychiatric nurse. It speaks volumes about Brother's heart that despite the cuts and bruises he suffered in the attack, his only concern was comforting me and making sure I was okay.

So when Grandma Ada was in her final days in the hospital, we were all diligent about seeing to it that Brother knew he would always be taken care of and adored just as his mother adored him. Late one night I came home from the hospital after a day at Grandma Ada's side and saw that the light was still on in Brother's room. I sat down beside him on his bed. He opened his eyes and searched my face for some kind of hope about the woman we both loved so much. I didn't have any to offer. What I did have, though, was Grandma Ada's treasured crucifix. A nurse had given it to me that afternoon, explaining that my grandmother wanted me to have it. I put it in the palm of Brother's transparent hand and closed his fingers around it.

"This should be yours," I whispered to him.

He shook his head and simply said, "I don't think I'll need it now." He put the crucifix back in my hand, and we cried together and recited the rosary.

When I came home from Grandma Ada's memorial service a few days later, I went to Brother's room to tell him all about it as I'd promised I would. I opened his door and walked toward his bed, managing a smile and saying, "Oh, Brother, she looked so beautiful. . . ."

That was as far as I got before Brother went into convulsions. He was rushed to the hospital and died two hours later. Left behind in his room were all his clothes and papers, perfectly organized in neat piles, the clothing carefully folded exactly as if he knew he was going home and had no intention of leaving a mess behind. The effort it must have taken him was unimaginable, but that loving, gentle soul wouldn't have had it any other way. What an honor to have known him, and what great peace there finally was in the certainty that he and Grandma Ada were at Home and together again, exactly where they belonged.

———

TWO DAYS LATER I was alone in my room, going through the motions of getting dressed, when I had the strongest feeling that someone was there with me. I glanced past my reflection in the dresser mirror and saw nothing but the closed bedroom door behind me. I turned and looked around. Still nothing. I focused on the mirror again, and now I was sure I felt a soft warm breath, just for an instant, passing across the back of my neck. I dismissed it as that word Grandma Ada always swore should be banished from the English language: *imagination.*

Two things happened almost simultaneously to prove me wrong: what sounded like a deafening clap of thunder filled the room as, crystal clear and unmistakable, Grandma Ada's voice said, "Sylvia!" Less than a second later silence thickened the air, as if an electrical storm had just blown through.

My heart pounding with fear, I raced out my bedroom door to find Daddy running up the stairs toward me.

"Sylvia, what the hell happened?" he shouted. "What was that horrible cracking noise? It sounded like the roof collapsed. Are you all right? You're white as a sheet."

I was trembling, and he put his arm around me, walked me back into my room and sat down next to me on the bed as I described the previous two or three minutes. It surprised me to see him smiling.

"What was it your grandmother promised you?" he reminded me. "Didn't she say she'd send you a sign when she got Home? I think she just kept her promise."

That deafening cracking noise, I learned later, was something called a "rapport," and it's not all that uncommon. Occasionally, when a spirit travels from the high-frequency dimension of the Other Side to our much lower frequency here on earth, it exceeds the speed of sound and creates shock waves, exactly the same sudden, intense buildups and releases of atmospheric pressure we experience as sonic booms. A rapport is simply the spirit world's version of a sonic boom. They've been reported and studied for thousands of years. But for all the countless spirit visits I've received, the only rapport I've ever experienced was the one that Grandma Ada created in my bedroom that day to tell me she'd made it Home safely. Leave it to her to reassure me with a sign I couldn't possibly miss.

––––––––––

GRANDMA ADA HAD insisted that someday I would be a teacher. Francine kept telling me that someday I would be a famous psychic and speak to large groups of people. It never occurred to me that those two predictions weren't mutually exclusive, and I much preferred Grandma Ada's. So I threw myself into my studies while also pursuing a very personal dream of my own, the most traditional, grounded, Norman Rockwell imagery you can imagine: a white picket fence surrounding a sweet little house, probably with bluebirds swooping down to trim my homemade pie crust, where I would spend my days as a school teacher and then hurry home to lovingly tend to my happy, handsome husband and darling children. I was determined to create a strong, secure, cohesive family and succeed where my parents had failed.

Early proof that Francine's right: none of us is allowed to read our own charts while we're here on earth, which is why there's not a psychic on earth, including me, who's psychic about themselves.

I had a lot of dates and a few serious boyfriends, none of them any more or less intense, heartbreaking, and ill conceived than yours probably were at that age. One wanted no part of this ridiculous psychic/Francine thing, or this nonsense about my going to college—I would hardly need a college education on the farm he dreamed of, raising our six children, for heaven's sake. (Picture that.) Another I was so crazy about that I'm sure I would have married him in a heartbeat, until I found out, not from him, that he already had a wife and children back east. Still another I genuinely loved, and he was a wonderful man. But it became unavoidably apparent that there would have been three of us kneeling at our wedding altar: him, the grim disapproving woman beside him, and me in my white gown and veil robotically pledging, "I, Sylvia, take you and your mother. . . ."

Agonizing as they seemed at the time, my relationship dramas paled in comparison to a crisis of the soul that had been building at school for several months. I'd become increasingly fascinated with the working of the human mind, and in addition to my required studies at St. Theresa's I eagerly signed up for a course in abnormal psychology as well as an evening hypnosis class at the University of Kansas City. I found them both mesmerizing, but before long that abnormal psychology textbook started shaking me to my core as I read symptom after symptom of the deeply disturbed mind and realized that many of them described me much too closely for my own comfort.

Seeing spirits and countless other images that no one else sees? You mean, that sign of various mental illnesses textbooks refer to as hallucinations?

Hearing disembodied voices, like, oh, Francine, for example? Not uncommon in schizophrenia and other severe psychological afflictions.

Picking up depression, fear, paranoia, and every other negative emotion in the book from crowds of people around me? How did I know those disturbances were originating in other people? What made me think they weren't all originating in me?

In other words, what if that three-hundred-year psychic family legacy Grandma Ada had taught me to cherish was actually a three-hundred-year family legacy of insanity?

The more I read, the more obvious it became: I wasn't psychic at all. I was nuts. And most certainly too nuts to be allowed anywhere near children, let alone teach them.

Once I'd diagnosed myself beyond any reasonable doubt, I made an appointment for a consultation with Dr. John Renick, who was a psychiatrist and one of my most brilliant, most trusted professors.

I also said an official, sarcastic good-bye to the imaginary alter ego called Francine I'd been deluding myself with every day for the past twelve years. "She" didn't argue, didn't defend herself, didn't even have the decency to get emotional. What she did do was ask me to allow her one indulgence before I permanently wrote her off as nothing more than a voice in my head.

"One indulgence? Like what?" I asked, feeling ridiculous talking to her.

"You've never seen me," she said. "I'll appear for you tonight."

I accepted the challenge, as much as the idea terrified me. At least when nothing happened, I would have all the sad proof I needed that my treasured friend, confidante, and Spirit Guide Francine never existed. I assembled my parents and sister for moral support and tried to ignore their excitement over the prospect of Francine materializing after all these years of my blathering about her. We could hear a night rain against the window as I dimmed the lights per Francine's instructions (to protect her eyes on her first trip to this dimension since 1520, she said), and we settled in to wait.

We didn't have to wait for long.

Almost imperceptibly the rocking chair beside me began to move, and the folds of a soft blue dress slowly took shape on the wood seat. Next came a hand with long, slender fingers, resting in the lap of the dress.

Daddy managed in an emotionally choked whisper, "Don't anyone say a word. We don't want to influence each other about what we're seeing." There was no danger of that. Except for the rain on the window, the silence in the room was almost palpable.

An arm the color of pale mocha formed above the hand, with a long black braid of hair resting against it.

That was all I could handle. I turned away and never glanced back, while my family, overwhelmed, kept on gaping. When they compared notes after it was over and Francine had disappeared, it was clear that they'd all seen exactly the same woman: tall, very thin, with perfect skin, huge dark doe eyes and high cheekbones, almost Egyptian looking and serenely beautiful. The whole experience of her, and of being in her presence, moved them to tears, while I couldn't get away from them fast enough and without saying a word left them to their awe.

I told Dr. Renick the whole story at our first therapy session the next day, and he was surprised at my reaction. My family and I had seen absolute proof that Francine was real, and her being real meant that I wasn't insane after all. He thought that would have been cause for celebration. "So why did you turn away from seeing her?"

Now it was my turn to cry as I blurted out, "Because I have to live in this world, Dr. Renick. I hear and see what normal people don't, and I'm supposed to be grateful for that because it's a gift from God. But I don't want to be some freak, some goofy, airy-fairy weirdo. I just want to be a teacher. I just want to be normal. That's all I want."

He gave me the kindest, most compassionate smile and replied, "What a perfectly sane thing to say."

I still have the piece of paper on which he wrote his diagnosis: "Normal, but has paranormal abilities?" Even with the question mark, it meant the world to me, and from that day forward I never doubted my gifts or my sanity.

THE WHITE PICKET FENCE

Now that I'd accepted Francine as a very real spirit from the Other Side who was apparently going to be with me for the rest of my life, I wondered if she could find a slower, lower-octave, less grating way of communicating with me and side-step the sound distortion between her dimension and mine. There was a way, she told me: I could trance her, so that she could channel her voice through me and my vocal cords. I wouldn't be conscious of anything she said while I was channeling her, but I could record it and play it back as often as I wanted.

Of course. How logical. And fat chance. I wasn't about to hand over control of my mind or any part of my body to anyone, Spirit Guide or not. Francine assured me that trancing was a risk-free exercise; it would never happen without my allowing it, and I could end the trance and reclaim control again whenever I wanted. Why not let her try it sometime if the opportunity presented itself and let her prove how harmless and potentially helpful it was?

I responded with, "Yeah, that'll happen," or something equally sarcastic, momentarily forgetting that Francine doesn't understand sarcasm and, in fact, interprets every communication precisely and literally. (For example, if you ask her, "Can you tell me what you look like?" she'll reply, "Yes." Technically a truthful answer, but if it's not what you were going for, you need to reword your request to, "Please tell me what you look like.")

Two nights later I was in hypnosis class. My old friend Mary Margaret was with me, along with thirty other students. I remember Dr. Royal "counting us down." The next thing I remember was regaining consciousness, not at my very loveliest. I'm double jointed, so I "awoke" to find myself still seated in my chair, bent forward as far as I could go, the top of my head resting on the floor, with everyone in the room gaping at me. Mortified, I sat up, trying unsuccessfully to affect an "I meant to do that" expression, and started to catch bits and pieces of the excited comments around me: "Was that for real?" . . . and, "Never heard anything like it . . ." and, "So much information! . . ." and the one that alerted me the most, "Like she was someone else!"

I turned helplessly to Mary Margaret, who simply whispered, "Francine was here. Talking through you."

For the rest of the evening I listened with some combination of chagrin and smoldering anger as Dr. Royal and my classmates described the half-hour while I was "gone." After introducing herself to the group, Francine launched into fascinating detail about the Other Side, reincarnation, Spirit Guides, the eternal journey of the soul, and, pardon the expression, God knows what else. There was unanimous agreement that even though it was my voice they were listening to, the speech patterns, the terminology, the rhythms, and everything else that came out of my mouth sounded absolutely nothing like me at all. And gee, here's good news: everyone loved her and wanted her to come back soon.

I exploded at Francine that night, feeling completely betrayed and demanding an explanation. She remained calm, patient, and logical as always while reminding me that (a) she said she'd be watching for an opportunity to channel through me; (b) she'd promised she would never channel through me against my will; (c) the hypnotic trance that made it possible for her to channel through me occurred with my permission; therefore (d) it was with my permission that she'd seized the opportunity. Besides, had I noticed that not one bit of harm had come to me from channeling her and that my classmates seemed to have benefited from the experience of meeting a full-fledged resident of the Other Side?

Have I mentioned that I've never won an argument with her?

I agreed to embrace the practice of channeling her, with a few nonnegotiable conditions: she would never surprise me again as she had in class that night; she would tell nothing but the absolute truth when speaking through me; she would never use my voice to cause harm to me or to anyone else; and I would only channel her for the highest possible service to God. And all these decades and trance sessions later, not once has she breached that agreement.

Make no mistake, there never has been and never will be a lecture or an appearance at which the audience is expecting me but gets Francine instead, or vice versa. There's a process I go through when I vacate my body, a feeling similar to, let's say, being anesthetized, deeply hypnotized, or very deeply asleep—I sit quietly, go into intense relaxation, and close my eyes; there are a few subtle jerks of my body as I "leave" and Francine "comes in," and from the moment that happens I have absolutely no awareness of what happens until she "leaves" and I "come back" again. From the footage I've seen, nothing more visibly dramatic happens than my eyes opening again, and my body sitting perfectly still, while my voice transmits Francine's speech patterns, slower and more deliberate than mine, with information and a vocabulary that are far more extensive than mine. I can give expert lectures (and do) about the spirit world and the Other Side as an eye- and ear-witness. What Francine offers by channeling through me are lectures from a current resident of the Other Side, and since I have nothing to do with those lectures and am not even "present" during them, I can say objectively after listening to countless tapes, she's absolutely, powerfully fascinating.

———————

I WAS NINETEEN when I graduated from St. Theresa's, and a month before my twentieth birthday I started my teaching career at a small parochial school in Kansas City. I was the only lay teacher there in a faculty of nuns. It wasn't just my first teaching job, it was my first job of any kind, and I was a nervous wreck. I changed outfits more often getting dressed for my first day than I had for any date in my life—somehow all the clothes I'd exhaustively shopped for, that seemed so appropriate and professional in the store, looked either too severe, too relaxed, or too frilly. I settled on a tweed suit that I thought Katharine Hepburn would have worn in this same situation, marched into my windowless basement classroom, and prayed that the fifty-five children staring at me from their desks weren't able to smell fear.

And thus began one of the most challenging, gratifying, worth-while experiences of my life. Just as Grandma Ada had predicted for so many years, teaching was where I belonged. She and Francine had also predicted that teaching would help prepare me for some bigger, more expansive calling, but I was happy right where I was, know-ing I was making a difference to children who didn't just need to be taught, they needed to be nourished, and heard, and cared about. I told them every day that I loved them, and they never doubted that.

They had a psychic teacher, but they never made an issue of it, never asked how I knew exactly what problems each of them had at home, who was abused, or neglected, or sleep deprived because their parents had fought all night, or in need of medical attention that their single parent couldn't afford, or in too chaotic a household to concen-trate on their homework. They simply accepted that Miss Shoemaker "knew things" and could be counted on to quietly pull a student aside for a private comforting talk when he or she needed it. I've always hoped that I gave those children a fraction as much as they gave me.

It was late one Friday afternoon. I was a few weeks into the job and just starting to feel less like a novice and more like a real live capable teacher. I finished grading papers, looked around the windowless classroom, and smiled at the Halloween decorations we'd made and put up that day. As I left, I was very careful to lock the door behind me as always. The principal, Sister Regina Mary, ran a tight ship. I admired her and respected her very much and even feared her a little—she was one of those people who could make your blood run cold with a single look.

So when Sister Regina Mary called me at home the next day, my first call from her on a weekend, sounding as if something was wrong, it was all I could do not to start whimpering, beg her not to fire me, and promise it would never happen again, whatever "it" was.

"I just had the strangest experience," she said, "and I'm hoping you can give me an explanation."

Oh, dear. An explanation. That's never good. "I'll certainly do my best, Sister," I promised her, so overly earnest that I even sounded guilty to myself.

"I came to my office this afternoon to catch up on paperwork, as I often do on Saturdays when I know no one else will be in the building and I won't be disturbed." Her voice started to tremble a little as she continued, "I thought I heard a noise downstairs. I dismissed it at first, because of course no one could possibly get in without setting off the alarm. I like to maintain a certain level of security." I smiled to myself with the passing thought that given a choice, I'd rather try to break into Fort Knox than into Sister Regina Mary's school.

"But the more I listened," she continued, "the more convinced I was that someone was walking around on the lower level. So I picked up my crucifix and went downstairs, and, Sylvia, the door to your classroom was standing open."

I don't mind getting in trouble when I've done something wrong, but I do mind when I'm being falsely accused. "Sister, you have my word, I locked that door when I left last night, I know I did."

"I know you did too. I checked every door before I went home, and there's no doubt about it, yours was locked, which is why I was so shocked to find it open this afternoon. I heard the footsteps again, coming from inside your classroom, and I walked to the door to confront the intruder."

"Who was it?" I asked, as concerned as she was now.

"A friend of yours, apparently. She was just looking around the room smiling, and she asked me to tell you that she thinks you're doing a wonderful job. I introduced myself, but she didn't give me her name, she simply said you'd know."

"What did she look like?"

"She was elderly, fairly tall, with pure white hair very stylishly arranged on top of her head. She had on a blue dress, and she smelled like fresh lavender." I held my breath, barely able to believe what I was hearing, as she went on. "What made it even more unnerving, and please don't think I'm crazy, but the phone rang, and I excused myself and stepped out into the hall to answer it. I was only gone for a few seconds, and I was right outside the door. But Sylvia, when I went back into the classroom again, she was gone."

"I'm not surprised," I said.

"You know this woman?"

"She's my grandmother."

"Then will you please explain to me how she got into a locked room and how she managed to leave without my seeing her?"

My motto: When in doubt, take a deep breath and just tell the truth. "It was easy for her, Sister. She's dead."

"I see," was all she said, at which point she suddenly remembered she was late for an appointment and hung up as quickly as her good manners would allow, while I basked in a glow of pure, undying love and could almost feel Grandma Ada's lavender-scented arms around me.

It was an affirmation that, from very close by on the Other Side,

Grandma Ada had my back, as did Francine. I had a job I loved. I had a united family, such as it was.

And I had a blind date with a policeman.

––––––––

MARY MARGARET WAS dating a policeman named Jerry, and Jerry was friends with an available fellow policeman who wanted to meet me. I was still mourning the breakup of my relationship with the wonderful boyfriend and his mother, a.k.a. She Who Must Be Obeyed, and a blind date on my birthday sounded like a nice distraction.

Gary Dufresne had grown up an Army brat, traveling with his family all over the world, attending high school in Japan. He then enlisted with the Marines, and after his four-year tour of duty he found his way to Kansas City, where he'd been with the police force for three years. He was tall and muscular, with azure eyes and a nice smile. I wasn't smitten at first sight. But I'd been down the smitten-at-first sight road a few times, and those didn't turn out so well.

I admit it: I was much more intrigued by the news that he'd been smitten with me at first sight two years earlier. He'd given a friend of mine a parking ticket, and—here's a surprise—I went on an outraged rant on her behalf, something about cops wasting time and taxpayers' money handing out tickets instead of apprehending criminals, and apparently I blurted out my name during my rant. I vaguely remembered the incident but had no memory of the cop involved. He, on the other hand, had been trying to track me down ever since and was shocked at the number of Shoemakers who lived in the Kansas City area. He was sure it was fate that we were reunited on a blind date, and at that stage of my personal life, I wasn't sure enough of anything any more to argue the point.

He was persistent, attentive, and self-assured. He and my parents liked each other. He had a stable, admirable job. He was a few years older and ready to settle down in Kansas City, as close to or far away from my family as I liked. He didn't put much stock in this "fortune-telling" thing of mine, but he didn't mind it either. He knew what he wanted, he wanted me, and I wanted to be wanted.

I still can't quite believe this made sense to me at the time—or, to put it more accurately, I still can't quite believe I charted this—but my blind date with Gary Dufresne was on October 19, 1958, and I married him at the St. James Church on April 2, 1959. I was so swept away with my parents' excitement and the preparations, shopping for invitations and a gown and bridesmaids' dresses and a caterer and a florist and a reception hall and an orchestra and, and, and, that I didn't get around to the inevitable breakdown until the night before the ceremony.

As always, Mary Margaret was with me in my bedroom as I sobbed into my pillow, "What am I doing? I don't love this man. I don't even know this man."

"I hate to say I told you so, but I think I've said the word 'rebound' at least three or four hundred times in the last few months. You just didn't want to hear it," she reminded me. "I'll bet Francine has been trying to talk you out of this too."

"All she keeps telling me is that everything will work out as it's meant to." I couldn't resist adding, "In other words, she's no help either."

She ignored that and pressed ahead with an urgency in her voice. "The good news is, you don't have to go through with this. You can call it off right now. I promise, Sylvia, it's not too late."

The sheer enormity of what calling it off would require, not to mention the disappointment I'd be inflicting on family and friends I loved, was suddenly more horrifying than the thought of going through with it. But all I said was, "Yes it is."

The ceremony and reception were a huge hit, crowded, pretty, and Midwest Catholic traditional. I have two crystal-clear memories of that afternoon: walking down the aisle on my father's arm, his beaming pride making me feel like the most beautiful bride in wedding history; and stealing a glance at Gary as we knelt in front of the priest and feeling a rush of emptiness when it hit me again that I was promising before God and these witnesses, for the rest of my life, to love, honor, and obey this stranger. And from the bottom of my heart, that was my intention, whatever it took. Like every other overachiever, I never accepted challenges with the idea in mind that failure was an option. Now that I'd vowed to be a wife, I was determined to be great at it.

Maybe Gary was doing his version of that—trying to be a great head of the household—because the minute he'd secured the title of husband, he became controlling, hypercritical, and volatile. He was in charge of everything from our finances to our social life to our television viewing habits to proper housekeeping methods to what time meals should be served, what we should eat, and how it should be cooked. I don't remember ever cleaning the house, cooking a meal, doing the laundry, dressing, or doing much of anything else to his satisfaction. The more he criticized the harder I tried, and the harder I tried the more he criticized. And on the rare occasions when I got fed up and became defiant, or committed some unforgivable sin like losing one of his socks in the dryer, he wouldn't hesitate to lose his temper and hit me, throw me around, or both.

We'd been married for about a month the first time it happened. I'd come home from the store, and as he watched me putting groceries away ("woman's work," you know) with increasing impatience, he finally asked where the hell his 7-Up was. I said, "Sorry. I forgot." And in the blink of an eye, he backhanded me across the mouth, splitting my lip open.

I don't have the vocabulary to describe how shocked, stunned, and horrified I was. I mean, I like 7-Up as much as the next person, but to smack someone over it . . . or over anything, for that matter?

Sadly, rather than recognizing the world's largest red flag, I immediately told myself it was an anomaly, he was just tired or stressed or something and it wouldn't happen again. Famous last words, of course. In fact, the cracked femur I'm limping from today, fifty years later, was the result of a high-speed collision between me and a rock-solid door jamb. And every step of the way I kept right on telling myself all the classic things battered women tell themselves: it will get better, he'll change, or—the biggest lie of all—I keep provoking him. Let's face it, as long as we keep blaming ourselves, we'll never get around to blaming the person who truly deserves it.

To the rest of the world, though, the School Teacher and the Policeman were an adorable couple. Gary's public persona was funny, charming, outgoing, and entertaining, and we had a lot of friends who loved to socialize. We were living in an apartment close to my family, so we saw them often too. They were enchanted with him and with my happy façade, and I was willing to move heaven and earth to keep from worrying or disappointing them with the truth.

I couldn't lie to Francine, of course, nor did I need to tell her what was going on—she was vigilantly watching it all unfold from her up-close-and-personal vantage point three feet away on the Other Side, but as always, she couldn't and wouldn't interfere. I'd charted this situation, after all, and it was mine to figure out. It would give me more wisdom for helping people later on, she would say without explaining, or she'd simply repeat over and over again, "What have you learned when times were good?" True enough, but not that helpful when all I really wanted was for someone who knew what was going on to tell me what to do about it.

At 9:30 p.m. on December 9, 1959, according to Francine, Gary and I conceived our first child. It was a boy, she said, who would someday become a six-foot-five-inch man.

I was ecstatic when my doctor confirmed my pregnancy. Gary, on the other hand, was furious, apparently taking the position that I'd conceived this child by myself. What was *I* thinking, putting a strain on our budget and tying us down with a baby like this, when we hadn't even been married a year? Was *I* just too stupid or unrealistic to understand what a bad idea this was, blah, blah, blah?

For the first time in our marriage, I frankly couldn't have cared less what he thought. I wanted a baby enough for both of us, and no amount of sulking on Gary's part was going to change that. As far as I was concerned, I gave him the most miraculous birthday gift a man could ever hope for: Paul Jon Dufresne was born a month early, on his father's birthday, August 19, 1960. If Gary would have preferred a funny barbecue apron or a Ping-Pong table, oh well.

Being a mother taught me a whole new meaning of the word *love*. It also taught me a whole new meaning of the words *sleep deprivation*. Paul was colicky and typically cried through the night, which made Gary even more volatile than he was before. Between the exhaustion and the constant stress, I was barely functioning by the time school started in the fall. I begged Gary to let me take a year off and stay home with our new baby, but that only proved to him yet again what an idiot I was—if I had a brain in my head, I would have known that we needed both our incomes to make ends meet, "you moron!" (It might have helped if I'd had a clue how much Gary was making, but he filed that information under "none of your business." And I, in keeping with my idealized, overachieving notion of how the Perfect Wife should behave, didn't run the risk of causing trouble and disrupting the household by demanding information he didn't volunteer.)

So I was back to school, and even found a couple of part-time jobs on the side to be absolutely sure I was holding up my end of the bargain. I thank God for my family right up the street for taking care of Paul while I worked and adoring him almost as much as I did. (Don't worry, I saw to it that he was never left alone with my mother.) I was still constantly exhausted, but I loved my new baby and I loved teaching, and despite Gary's long hours and growing disinterest in being home at all, I had little glimmers of hope that maybe life was starting to smooth itself out.

You would think I'd have learned by then not to exhale, wouldn't you?

When Paul was five months old, he fell victim to a staph infection that had become an almost citywide epidemic. His fever soared to 105°, and I bundled him up and floored it to the hospital, promising him that I wasn't about to let him die and wishing I had the power to see to it that I kept that promise. He went straight into intensive care, where he stayed for the next twenty-six hours. I kept my family away, afraid that they'd become infected too, and Gary was working a double shift of thirty straight hours on duty, so I spent every minute of those twenty-six hours alone in the waiting room— without so much as a peep of reassurance from Francine.

I asked for her help so often in that waiting room that it sounded like a mantra, adding that this was *not* the time to hit me with her line about everything working out the way it was meant to. If she didn't have anything more specific than that to offer, I wasn't interested. Her silence in response did nothing but add to my fear, as I filled in the blanks myself and assumed that she knew I couldn't handle hearing what she had to say about Paul and, being incapable of lying to me, was choosing to say nothing instead. Again, it's not a Spirit Guide's job to intervene in anyone's chart; they're just with us to guide, so beyond silently seeing to it that I caught onto Paul's illness immediately and got him to the hospital in record time, Francine's primary responsibilities for this crisis had already been taken care of. (Even I, knowing everything I know, can mistakenly find myself wishing that Francine could magically transform herself into Wonder Woman every once in awhile.)

My countless prayers to God were answered, though. Paul's fever broke, he started recovering, and a week later I was able to bring him home. Once he was safely asleep in his own crib again, I confronted Francine, demanding to know how she could leave me at the most terrifying time in my life when I'd never needed her more. I was afraid my precious child was dying, and she was nowhere to be found?

"Is that what was going on?" she answered with her infuriating serenity. "I knew something was wrong, but I had no idea what it was. I can't read your mind, you know."

No. I didn't know. I guess I assumed she could. I guess I assumed she knew everything about me, whether I communicated it or not. But the truth is, Spirit Guide or not, her reaction to my pleading to her for help with no explanation was not unlike what your reaction or mine would be to our best friend calling, yelling, "Help!" and then hanging up without a word about what they needed. We'd be just as stumped as Francine was. As for my prayers, she explained that those were between me and God, and nothing she had access to.

It was a good lesson for me, and let it be a lesson for you as well: when talking to your Spirit Guide, as I hope you'll do regularly, *be specific about what you need from them at that moment!* (By the way, even if you don't believe a word of this whole Spirit Guide thing, talk to yours anyway. If I'm telling the truth—and I am—it will profoundly enrich your life. If I'm wrong, what possible harm can it do?)

Paul's recovery was only the beginning of some long overdue good news in the Dufresne household. From the moment he came home from the hospital, Paul began sleeping straight through the night, which meant that I began sleeping straight through the night, and the relief of feeling rested and healthy again was exhilarating. I finally had enough energy for all three of my jobs, my full-time homemaking responsibilities, and the honor (not too strong a word) of being a mother.

Then there was Gary's announcement that, thanks entirely to him (apparently I was working three jobs just for the hilarious fun of it), we'd saved enough money to buy a house of our own, in a new subdivision of tract homes that were under construction. I was ecstatic. No more being packed like sardines into our little apartment, Paul would have an official nursery of his own rather than having his crib act as the footboard of his parents' bed, and maybe when we weren't living virtually on top of each other Gary's chronic misery would fade away into suburban contentment. I made a mental note to myself to start pricing white picket fences.

We walked through the available model houses, Gary chose the one he liked, and I pretended to prefer that one too. He handed over the deposit, I sat down at a pile of paperwork as tall as I was and mindlessly signed here, here, here, here, here, and here, and a month later we stepped for the first time into our newly completed trilevel home, just like a real family.

The instant we were inside the door I was overwhelmed with such a wave of sheer dread that I felt as if my knees were going to buckle under me. I grabbed Gary's arm for support and said, "Something's very wrong in this house."

He looked around and proclaimed, "Nothing's wrong. It's perfect."

I desperately wanted that to be the case, but I knew better. "Gary, I'm telling you, we don't belong here. Something's wrong, and we don't belong here. Can't you feel that?"

"Don't even think about starting that spook crap with me," he ordered. "I've got a nonrefundable deposit and a bank loan that says we *do* belong here, so shut up and start getting these boxes unpacked."

Again, I can't stress enough, I wanted this to work—this house, this family, this whole dream. And I gave it all I had and then some. He'd seemed "on paper" like a good idea at the time I agreed to marry him—he was a solid and reliable breadwinner, my parents more than approved, he claimed to want children as much as I did, and so what if I wasn't in love with him? But there are some forces that are just plain bigger than "all I had," and they were relentless in their efforts to let us know how unwelcome we were. As I came to discover, we were intruding on someone else's property.

Paul's nursery was adorable, bright and cheerful with yellow and white wallpaper and sky-blue furniture I painted myself. Unfortunately, he never spent a single night in it. He started screaming in terror the moment I set foot in that room with him, and putting him in his crib was tantamount to torturing him. There was no way around it; it was back to his parents' bedroom for Paul and his crib.

We were now the proud owners of a beautiful German shepherd named Thor, who made it immediately apparent that he wanted no part of Paul's nursery or any other room in that house either. The fur on his back would stand straight up and he would start growling, seemingly at nothing, a thousand times a day, and one night we witnessed some unseen force picking him up and throwing him across the room into the screen door. (He was desperately frightened but otherwise fine, thank God.)

I became very ill, and when I finally gave in and consulted a doctor he took one look at my oddly yellow eyes and urgently checked me into the hospital. The diagnosis was acute hepatitis, and before I knew it I was being wheeled into an operating room for five hours worth of surgery to remove part of my liver, gall bladder, and intestines. To Gary's thorough exasperation I was ordered not to work for a month after I was released from the hospital, putting an unexpected strain on whatever financial shape we were in.

Gary was rarely home—work or something (another one of those "none of your business" topics)—and I asked my sister Sharon to spend the night with me while I was still recovering from surgery. We walked into my bedroom to put Paul to sleep in his crib and found ourselves gaping at three images that had appeared out of no-

where on the wall above my dresser: a half moon, a star, and a shape
that vaguely resembled a swastika, all in an eerie glowing blue. We
both tried to write them off as reflections of . . . shapes resembling
absolutely nothing around us, caused by light from . . . uh . . . nothing, since it was completely dark in the room. From that night on,
the shapes, which disappeared during the day, appeared like clock-
work just after dusk. Sharon and I never did uncover the "perfectly
logical explanation" for why and how they got there. I'd seen more
than my share of apparitions in my life, but these glowing emblems
on the wall sent a chill up my spine.

"Ask Francine," Sharon suggested, and I nominated myself for that
year's Village Idiot award. I'd been so consumed with the turbulence
around me that I hadn't thought of that.

"This house is standing on sacred Indian burial ground," was
Francine's answer. "Your intrusion is sacrilege. You will never be at
peace here."

After a lot of searching, I found a yellowed land grant and map at the
library that confirmed Francine's information. I also found drawings of
that swastika-like shape in a book of Native American symbols.

I shared this startling burial ground news with Gary, whose take
on it was, "So what? I'm sure someone's buried pretty much everywhere. Where are we supposed to live, in midair?"

There was no getting through to him, but an upcoming flurry of
events took care of that for me.

First, a tornado hit our house, and only ours; the houses on either
side of us were untouched. The damage was minimal, and I was
grateful for that, but by then it felt a little beside the point.

Then Gary stopped working for the police force and was unem-
ployed for a time.

Next, just as we finished repairing the tornado damage, the house
caught fire. The cause: undetermined. This time the damage was
more extensive, but there were no injuries.

The night of the fire Gary called an old friend, a fellow cop who'd relocated to join the Sunnyvale, California, police department. After a few minutes of bringing him up to date on recent events, Gary asked if there might be an opening on the force in Sunnyvale. Moments later he covered the mouthpiece of the phone and said, "Hey, Sylvia, Don says he's sure he can get me a job. . . ."

I didn't hear the rest of the sentence. I was already packing.

Six weeks later, when the school year and my teaching responsibilities were finished, Gary, Paul, Thor, and I were on our way to California. I knew I would desperately miss my family and friends in Kansas City. But as high a price as that was to pay, it seemed worth it for the sheer relief of escaping that house.

I eventually found out that what we experienced in our shiny new trilevel tract house was something called an "imprint." But that discovery was still many years and a whole other marriage away.

———————

LOOKING BACK, I'M willing to believe that as abusive and just plain disastrous as my marriage was, I probably charted it as the only way I could have received the blessings of my sons (Christopher Michael Dufresne was born on February 19, 1966) and the move to northern California, where I don't doubt for a moment I was supposed to be.

Not that things went smoothly when Gary, Paul, Thor, and I arrived. There was no opening for Gary on the Sunnyvale police force after all, so we limped along as best we could on my salary from my new teaching position at St. Albert the Great Elementary School in nearby Palo Alto. Gary's mood darkened, and while I continued to be the best homemaker I knew how to be, I was getting less and less invested in playing a game he'd made it clear I couldn't win no matter how hard I tried. Being Paul's mother and making sure he was loved and cared for was much more important to me, which Gary resented and for which I never did and never will apologize.

It was seemingly just another Saturday morning six weeks after we moved that the doorbell rang and I opened it to find Daddy, Mother, and Sharon standing there grinning at me. "Surprise!" they yelled in unison. I can count on less than one hand the number of times I've been rendered speechless in my life. That was one of those times. I don't think I moved or even blinked for several minutes while they hugged me hello and began carrying a suspiciously large number of suitcases into the living room.

Don't misunderstand, I'd had my share of separation pangs since I left them behind in Kansas City. I worried about them, I felt guilty about moving so far away, and I missed Daddy terribly. But I didn't miss the peacemaker role I'd evolved into among the three of them and their almost constant problems and dramas, probably because I had my hands full with the constant problems and dramas in my own marriage. (Trust me, by that time I knew I was in no position to throw stones.) So overall, I appreciated those six weeks of getting my bearings and trying to pull my own life into some kind of reasonable shape.

And now, here they were in my living room in Sunnyvale, California. "Surprise!" indeed, and with so many suitcases, too, I thought as I watched their ecstatic reunion with Paul.

But wait. There's more. They hadn't just come for a visit, they gleefully announced. Daddy had resigned his job, they'd sold their house, and they were moving in with us. I wasn't sure whether to laugh, cry, or run screaming. In the meantime, Gary was delighted—his allies had arrived, presumably ready to pitch in with all those things that were of no interest to him, like caring for his son, keeping his wife company, and helping around the house while sharing expenses when our money was, to put it politely, low.

Of course I stayed, and so did they, and we all lived together for a year. Even now, I have no idea how, but I do know that I twisted myself into a pretzel to create the illusion of the solid marriage they were counting on for me and from me. Several months into that year Gary got a job with the local fire department, and his long work hours away from home made the illusion easier to pull off. (What's the old saying—"For better or worse, but not for lunch"?) The two families finally "separated" by buying a duplex and living beside each other.

It was during that year that I learned something about my mother that probably explained a lot of her behavior (without for a moment excusing it). Our relationship as two adult women had evolved into what I can only describe as noncombative coexistence—I'd long since abandoned the idea that maybe someday we would like each other and instead settled into the luxury of being virtually immune to her, and the feeling was probably mutual. With one major exception we'll discuss later, I didn't care enough any more to try to avoid her, or even be discourteous to her, because it would have meant "engaging," and I'd had twenty-plus years of education on what a futile exercise that was. Sometimes there's great peace to be found in apathy.

So one day, while we were all wedged together in that tiny apartment, Mother asked me to stop by our friendly neighborhood drug store to pick up a prescription for her, the words, "While you do what?" may have entered my mind, but they didn't escape my mouth. I added it to my list of errands and headed out the door.

Imagine my surprise when I asked for the prescription and our friendly neighborhood pharmacist came out from behind the counter and pulled me aside for a private chat.

Unbeknownst to me, for who knows how many years, my mother had been indulging in an addiction to methedrine, which the pharmacist explained to me was the strongest prescription speed on the market, known to make its users edgy, incredibly short-tempered, and tense to the point of jaw-grinding, then plummet into nosedives that could keep them in bed for days. This particular bottle had been ordered for my mother by her doctor in Kansas City, and she'd begun doctor shopping in San Jose. "If she keeps this up," the pharmacist told me, "her heart will explode."

I confronted her, of course, but she told me to mind my own business. And except for calling her Kansas City doctor and threatening him with criminal charges if he ever called in another prescription for her, that's pretty much all I did. It's not how I would handle it today, now that society and I are so much better educated about prescription drug addiction and there are so many more resources available. But at the time, I had no idea where to start, I didn't want to upset Daddy by telling him when he would have felt as helpless about it as I did, and even if I'd known what to say or do, I was the last person on earth she would have listened to. Other than privately realizing that I'd just been given an answer to a whole lot of questions about my mother, I left her to her addiction, and her only response to my confronting her was to pick up her own prescriptions from then on.

————

NOWHERE ALONG THE way during all the drama and crises at home did I lose my passion for teaching and for learning, and toward both ends I enrolled in the English literature master's program at San Francisco University. It was there that I met one of the most significant men in my life. His name was Bob Williams, and he was my creative writing professor. We liked each other, we liked James Joyce, particularly *Ulysses*, and we began meeting at the campus coffee house after class to discuss literature and to get to know each other.

Bob was my first real friend in California—a close, strictly platonic friend and confidant, the first person on the West Coast I told about my being psychic and about Francine. He was intrigued, so much so that he asked if I would give him a reading. I wasn't wild about the idea, but I wasn't about to turn down a friend. When I arrived at the agreed-upon time and place, I found Bob waiting with two of his friends who were just as intrigued as he was and wanted readings too. There was no graceful way out of it and no real way to complain about doing something for Bob that came as naturally to me as breathing.

Apparently the readings were credible, because when the next creative writing class assembled, Bob, without warning, announced, "Mrs. Dufresne will now demonstrate her psychic gifts by giving readings to any of you who'd like to volunteer." There were fifty-two students in the class, and fifty-two hands went up. After a few initial twinges of irritation with Bob for blowing my cover, I have to say I thoroughly enjoyed every minute of it, and my classmates were very vocal about the fact that they did too.

Inevitably, those fifty-two told fifty-two others, and so on, and so on, and so on, and before long I was speaking and doing readings for every women's club, men's group, and service organization in Sunnyvale. I also volunteered to do readings for the local police and firefighters and was pleasantly surprised to find long lines waiting to see me.

Even the young, handsome captain of the Stanford University Fire Department showed up for an especially memorable session.

I knew psychically that his marriage would be ending soon, and while it made him sad, he wasn't surprised—apparently he and his wife had both worn themselves out trying to ignore the blameless truth that they'd both given up on the relationship, to the point where they didn't even care enough to fight about it, or for it, any more.

The good news was, I clearly saw that very soon he'd find a tall, red-haired woman who'd be very good for him, and they'd go into a successful, fulfilling business together. But for the first and only time during a reading, no matter how hard I tried, I couldn't see the woman's face. We tossed around a few jokes about why that might be happening—maybe she didn't have one, or maybe he wasn't ready to hear that she had a face like a foot. The fact remained, though, that he left in search of a tall redhead with a blank space between her bangs and her neck, and I watched him leave wondering why all of a sudden my psychic eye for detail had failed me.

One afternoon, instead of our usual trip to the coffee shop, Bob took me to a tiny out-of-the-way bookstore near campus, a treasure trove of secondhand and hard-to-find books by everyone from theosophist Madame Helena Blavatsky to psychic healer Edgar Cayce to Bertrand Russell and Jean-Paul Sartre.

I was in heaven, moving almost reverently from one aisle to the next like the kid in a candy store. Bob let me browse for several minutes before asking, "Ready for your assignment?"

"My assignment?" I was intrigued and having a great time. "Absolutely. What is it?"

"See these books on philosophy, metaphysics, and the paranormal? I want you to read every single one of them."

He didn't see this coming, but it was the truth: "I already have." My college studies in theology and psychology, combined with my voracious appetite for reading, my intense curiosity, and my lifetime of direct contact with the spirit world had naturally evolved into explorations of spirituality without my even realizing I'd gone there.

"Then read them again," he grinned. "But this time, do something with them. Don't just let them inspire you, let them activate you. Study. Teach. Broaden your horizons. With your gifts, these brilliant authors, and your willingness to learn, there's nothing you can't do. You could even start your own research foundation, to help separate the truth from the nonsense and then spread the word. Your work could be as important and as groundbreaking as you'll let it be." I was staring at him, more energized than I'd been in years. He gave me a tight, loving hug and added, "I believe in you. Just do it. I'll help you, you have my word."

He promised we'd start making plans as soon as he got back from a trip he'd committed to months earlier.

"Where are you going?" I asked.

The instant he said, "Australia," my heart sank and my blood ran cold. I was as surprised as he was when I blurted out that he couldn't go, that if he did he wouldn't make it back alive.

He took me seriously, but his round-trip plane ticket and his hotel deposit were nonrefundable. So, swearing he'd be careful, he left for Australia, and came home in a pine box, dead from advanced but undiagnosed lymphatic cancer. I was devastated, and I promised him that I would honor his memory and commit myself to the assign-ment he gave me that day in the bookstore.

I kept that promise. I became an even more voracious reader than I'd been before, absorbed every book on philosophy, metaphysics, theology, and the paranormal I could find, actively pursued speaking engagements at which I could channel Francine, and gave readings in every spare moment I had. I took a new teaching position at San Jose's Presentation High School, and I was ecstatic to be pregnant with my second son, not anticipating that my family was about to expand even before Chris would be born.

For a year or so I'd noticed a woman in the neighborhood who, to put it politely, wasn't discreet about the fact that she had a severe drinking problem, particularly when she'd go reeling across the street, oblivious to traffic, to replenish her alcohol supply at our local market. Occasionally I'd see her with her precious little daugh-ter Mary, whose well-being I worried about and whom I always made a fuss over when I ran into her, to make sure she knew that someone cared and thought she was special.

That casual history hardly prepared me for the morning during my pregnancy with Chris when I answered the doorbell to find

Mary and her already inebriated mother standing there. The conversation wasn't much more complicated than this:

MARY'S MOTHER: "Hi. I'm sure you recognize us from up the street. I've noticed that you're always very sweet to my child, and she's become very fond of you. My husband and I are going through a rough time trying to take care of her and her disabled older brother, and we wondered if she could live with you until we're back on our feet again."

ME: "Okay."

I took the extra precaution of being appointed Mary's legal guardian, and so it was that shortly before Chris was born, Paul got a four-year-old sister. She was with us until she left at the age of nineteen to get married. She's still part of the family, still takes care of her disabled brother, still travels with me whenever possible, and I couldn't love her more or consider her more my own daughter if I'd given birth to her myself.

Gary was so detached from all of us by then that he barely seemed to notice Mary's arrival, or Chris's birth, for that matter. Based on nothing but a grim determination to ignore everything I knew about the miserable human being I'd been married to for thirteen years, I'd told myself twenty or thirty thousand times since our move to California that Gary's oppressive moodiness and anger would disappear like magic when he started working again. But what do you know, he started working again, this time at the local fire department, and he was still oppressive, moody, and angry. Go figure. And I shudder to imagine how much longer I would have gone on being a numb, resigned, abused Stepford wife if one day Gary hadn't crossed a line I never saw coming.

He'd flown into one of his random rages over God knows what when suddenly, from across the room, I saw him raise his hand to

Paul. That had never happened before, and I'd be damned if it was ever going to happen again. I raced over to shield Paul from Gary's fist, took the hit, then turned on Gary and said, "Touch my children and I will kill you."

For the first and only time in our lives together, Gary was afraid of me. Frankly, he should have been. He responded by storming off into the bedroom, slamming the door behind him.

I, on the other hand, at the age of thirty-five, with my foster daughter and two sons, my purse, sixteen dollars and some loose change in my wallet (what bank accounts existed were solely in Gary's name, and I had no access to them), and the clothes on my back, walked out of the house and never felt a moment of regret.

THREE

FOR SALE: ONE USED WHITE PICKET FENCE

My children and I fled straight to my sister Sharon's house. By then she'd married a man named Richard who was in the airline industry. The newlyweds were exactly as excited as you'd think to find a relative and her three children on their doorstep, but when I gave them the headlines of what had happened and promised I'd find us our own place as soon as humanly possible, they didn't turn us away.

Obviously, moving into my parents' house wasn't an option. Not only were they still sharing a duplex with my estranged husband, but they were also heartbroken by my decision to leave Gary. They'd loved having me and their two grandsons living on the other side of our common wall. And I'd created such a convincing illusion of a happy marriage to keep them from worrying that they thought I'd lost my mind walking out on such a "fine man and father." I didn't want to hurt them by confessing that I'd been putting on a charade for the past thirteen years, and I could hardly blame them for being shocked at my behavior—with no more information than they had, thanks to me, of course it seemed shocking. So I shouldered my way through their disapproval, confident that sooner or later they'd figure Gary out for themselves and that there was too much love between Daddy and me to keep us apart forever.

The most discouraging aspect of my life at that point was my inability to find the right new home for me and my sons. "All I wanted" was something affordable, that would accept children, that would have an accessible fenced area for them to play in, and that was at least within a few miles of a reliable, reputable babysitter. I didn't think that list of requests was so unreasonable, but judging by the responses from one potential landlord after another, I might as well have been asking for a free mansion with its own staff, live-in chef, stables, and liveried chauffeur. As I fell face down into bed every night after another unsuccessful day of house hunting, Francine would say, "Don't worry, Sylvia, the perfect home is waiting for you." But would she tell me where I might find it, or when? Of course not. I ranked it right up there with her perpetual "Everything will work out as it's meant to" reassurance on my list of Useless Bits of Wisdom.

Making my children and me even less appealing as houseguests was Gary's incomprehensible habit of showing up from time to time, always late at night, and standing in the street yelling such threats as, "I'm going to kill the next one of you that walks out that door!" I assume he'd taken up drinking again and expanded it into a hobby; I just didn't understand, nor do I understand now, what he was trying to accomplish. If his goal was to frighten and upset the children, it worked. If it was to convince me to come back to him, he couldn't have found a more effective way to confirm that I'd done exactly the right thing by leaving.

We called the police on him, needless to say, but especially back then, calling the cops on a former cop wasn't exactly destined for success. They would show up, do their best to calm him down, point out that as long as he was standing in the street, a.k.a. public property, we couldn't have him arrested for trespassing, and they would inevitably escort him home and put him to bed. One cop who was clearly not a fan of Gary or of his behavior won my heart on his fourth or fifth trip to the house when he subtly gave me a look and whispered, "You know, if you pull him inside and shoot him as an intruder, you won't be prosecuted." He was kidding, but only a little. And I thought for the thousandth time in my life that being the devout pacifist I am is endlessly rewarding, but that doesn't mean it's always convenient.

WE'D BEEN LIVING with Sharon and Richard for about three months when an affordable apartment—a tenement—became available, and Paul, Chris, Mary, and I moved in with the modest funds I'd scraped together from the three jobs I continued to work. I was so eager for the children not to feel as poor as we really were that when they asked, "What's all that green stuff in the pool?" I cheerfully answered, "Water lilies," rather than the far more truthful "Algae." Fortunately, they never demanded an explanation about why I refused to let them go swimming in that pool full of water lilies.

My sons were already showing signs of becoming as different from each other as Sharon and I had been. Paul was outgoing, hilariously funny, very social, loved sports, and, other than volunteering that he knew he had a Spirit Guide named Timothy, had no curiosity about his psychic gifts or much of anything to do with the psychic or paranormal world.

Chris was more of an introvert, more sensitive, loved sports like his brother but was as comfortable with his psychic gifts as Paul was disinterested in his. Chris was especially fond of astral travel (his spirit taking little trips away from his body, whether he was awake or asleep), even when he was a toddler. He would be sitting beside me on the couch so peacefully, and at some point I would realize he was a little *too* peaceful. I'd look to the shag carpet in the room and sure enough, while his body never moved a muscle, I'd see tiny footprints in the rug from his spirit escaping to trot off and play. All it took to retrieve him was a stern, "Chris, get back here!" He'd respond, back in his body again, with the sweetest, most innocent smile any child has ever given his mother.

Like most children, Chris routinely played with spirits and Angels, and he met and accepted his Spirit Guide, Charlie, years younger than I was when I ran screaming from Francine the night she introduced herself. His favorite otherworldly playmate for awhile was Joey, who particularly touched his heart. When I asked Chris to tell me about his new friend, he started with, "Joey's all burned." That prompted our first talk about the difference between spirits and ghosts, one of which is that ghosts haven't found their way Home to heal yet; Joey was a ghost and needed our help to go to the Other Side where his family was waiting for him. I was so proud of Chris's sensitivity and unselfishness when he immediately understood and loved his friend enough to not just help him go but be happy for him when he said good-bye.

———————

ONE AFTERNOON I answered the phone to hear a pleasant male voice ask, "Is this Sylvia Dufresne?" When I confirmed that it was he continued, "I just had to call and let you know that you were right, my marriage is over."

I was a complete blank. "I know the feeling. Who is this?"

"You did a reading for me at the Stanford fire house, and you told me my wife and I would be splitting up." I still wasn't making the connection until he added, "I'm the one who's supposed to be meeting the tall redhead with no face."

"Of course," I said. I suddenly had total recall of that half-hour with the handsome young fireman. So much had happened since that it seemed like a lifetime ago, but did I mention how handsome he was? "You're Dal Brown."

By the time we finished the conversation we'd made a dinner date for that night. I still remember how intently he stared at me when I walked toward the small table at the restaurant where he was already waiting. He stood to greet me and hold my chair.

"I am who you were expecting, right?" I asked, self-consciously. "The way you were staring at me, I wasn't sure."

He was still staring as he sat down across from me. "I'm sorry," he told me. "I just hadn't remembered how tall and redheaded you are."

It hit me like a ton of bricks. The woman in Dal's reading whose face I couldn't see was the one woman whose chart I'm not allowed to read in this lifetime. The face I couldn't see was mine.

Dal and I quickly began a serious relationship, and in many ways he was a Godsend. He and my children never particularly bonded, but they were comfortable with each other. I, in the meantime, thrived in the transition from an ex-husband who made me feel I couldn't do anything right to this new, attentive, generous man who made me feel there was nothing I couldn't do and who respected and accepted my gifts—after all, we met because he came to me for a psychic reading that turned out to be accurate, so the resistance-skepticism ship had long since sailed. I'd walked on eggshells for so many years with Gary that the solid ground of Dal's world was a relief it took me awhile to trust. I gladly learned, though, and when Dal and I both found ourselves officially and legally divorced on January 4, 1972, we celebrated by getting married in a small, sweet, no-frills ceremony in Reno, Nevada.

My parents did not attend. They didn't just disapprove, they'd been shocked, furious, and disgusted with me since the day I walked out on Gary and were clinging to the hope that any day now I would come to my senses and return to the cozy duplex where I belonged. That hope died for them when I married this stranger, this intruder who was such a bad influence on their daughter that he'd managed to seduce me into recklessly throwing away my marriage and separating my sons from their (imaginary) loving, attentive father.

As upset as I knew they were, though, I still wasn't prepared for the call that came one day from my attorney. It was no surprise that Gary had decided to launch a lame, futile effort to have Paul and Chris taken away from me. What stunned me to the core of my soul was the news that, according to a phone conversation between my mother and my lawyer, my parents were threatening to testify on Gary's behalf if the case ended up in a courtroom.

I'd never felt so devastated or so betrayed. I couldn't eat, what little sleep I got was filled with nightmares, I cried myself sick, and more than once I was desperate enough that I had long talks with Dal about packing up the children some night and disappearing with them back to Kansas City or somewhere . . . anywhere. . . .

After a couple of weeks of this agony, I couldn't contain myself any longer, no matter how much my lawyer cautioned me against contacting my parents in a rage and potentially making things worse. I picked up the phone and called Daddy, starting with, "How dare you . . . ?!" and heading straight downhill from there.

I insist on believing that in less turbulent times, with a clearer, calmer head, I would have guessed this immediately: Daddy had no idea what I was talking about. He knew nothing about Mother's call to my lawyer. There was no "we" in the threat to help separate me from my children. Hell would freeze over before he would ever side with Gary against me to have Paul and Chris taken away, and he was genuinely horrified that Mother had even suggested such a thing. I don't know exactly what the conversation was when he hung up and confronted her, but I admit I'm sorry I missed it.

As it turned out, the case never went to court. My sons stayed with me, we all stayed with Dal, and I continued to pray that someday, when Daddy met Dal and saw that I really had made a healthy, positive choice for me and my children, we could truly be a family again.

As a long-delayed postscript to that story, many years later I remember looking over at Paul's wedding reception to see Mother and Gary merrily whirling around together in the middle of the dance floor. It didn't make me angry, or even upset me. I just smiled a little to myself and thought, "It makes the dark ones so much easier to keep track of when they clump up like that."

―――――――

DAL KICKED OFF our lives together by moving us out of the tenement and into a townhouse. He then sat me down one night and announced that because I'd been working so hard for so long, and because we could afford it, he thought it was about time that I took a year off. I made him repeat that three times before I was convinced that I'd heard him correctly. It was a fantasy I'd never bothered to express because I never thought it was a possibility, but I leapt at it when he offered and I cherished every second of it. I completed the hypnosis classes I'd begun in Kansas City, became certified, and logged enough hours to earn "master hypnotist" status. I devoured more books on philosophy, theology, metaphysics, and the paranormal than I could count. I spent endless hours talking to Francine, who was welcome and respected in this home. I studied. I researched. I dreamed. And I became great pals with my smart, funny, growing children. Dal worked long hours and always made sure I knew how much he loved coming home to me, and I wondered more than once why I'd spent so many years postponing my happiness rather than insisting on it.

I made such great progress in my emotional healing, in fact, that one day at my insistence, at a time when we knew Gary would be at work, Dal and I showed up at my parents' door with no warning to talk things through and try to take a few tentative steps toward reconciling. It turned out to be a testament to the powers of communication, love, and Gary's inability to keep his vindictiveness hidden forever. They learned that I was thriving; that I'd missed them (Daddy) terribly; that we would never deny them access to their grandchildren and wanted them involved in their lives; and that Dal was not some evil, sneering, moustache-twirling villain after all. He was just a friendly, easygoing man who genuinely adored their daughter. I learned that Daddy was lonely and struggling with his estrangement from the daughter he'd always called the light of his life; that waking up every morning with no purpose to look forward to was diminishing his customary health and joy; that their initial resistance to Dal had been just a manifestation of their fear of losing me; and that Gary had alienated Daddy forever by asking him for a $30,000 loan to hire a lawyer for his custody battle against me. (Daddy would give a stranger the shirt off his back, but he *never* handed over cash, even when the purpose didn't offend him as much as Gary's did.) There were a lot of tears, a lot of apologies, and a lot of hugs during that visit, and by the time we left I thought my heart would burst from the peace, relief, and elation of having my daddy back again.

I was blessed with another reunion a few days later that I'll remember all my life. There I was, home alone in domestic bliss, cooking a major dinner for the whole family, including Daddy and Mother, when I managed to start a grease fire. I was so panicked and determined to put it out that I inhaled much too much heavy black smoke without realizing it and didn't understand until dizziness set in that I was suffocating. Gasping for air, I bailed out of the kitchen, staggering as fast as I could toward the open sliding glass doors that led to the balcony about twenty feet away. About halfway there I knew I was going to pass out before I got there.

I fell forward, but before I hit the floor I was tackled from behind and hurled forward into the fresh outdoor air.

As I lay on the balcony on my stomach taking long, deep breaths, still in too much shock to wonder what happened or what or whose weight was on top of me, a thick long curl of blonde hair brushed across my shoulder from behind for an instant. Then I felt the weight vanish, and when I sat up and looked around the balcony and inside toward the lingering smoke, I was surprised to find that I was completely alone. Whoever saved me had to have come from the Other Side.

I knew it couldn't have been Francine who rescued me—her hair was jet black and straight, not blonde and softly curled. My next thought was that it might have been one of my Angels, since we all come here with Angels of our own, and they're known to be heroic and then disappear when their job is done without ever saying a word.

But no, Francine told me, it wasn't an Angel. It was Grandma Ada who'd come rushing from Home to save my life.

I impatiently pointed out to her that Grandma Ada's hair was white.

"It was blonde when she was thirty," she said. "All spirits on the Other Side are thirty years old."

"Why are they all thirty?"

Considering all the years I'd been communicating with her, I should have seen this answer coming: "Because they are."

I couldn't argue with that.

Just to clarify, usually when loved ones come to visit from Home, they appear at the age they were when you last saw them, so that you'll be sure to recognize them. An infant, or an elderly person who passed away, for example, might seem like a stranger to you if they showed up as a thirty-year-old; they want nothing more than for you to know who they are, and that they're blissfully healthy, happy, and watching over you. But apparently, in this emergency, Grandma Ada had no time to transform herself into the old woman she was when I said good-bye to her (not to mention that my recognizing her was beside the point in that situation).

———

So I was a lucky, happy, confident, well-read, energized woman when, toward the end of my year's sabbatical, Dal and a group of friends and I went to a lecture by a psychic who was famous at the time. (This psychic is still alive, so I have no intention of offending the person by naming names.) The longer I sat there, the more infuriated I became with what I was hearing, to the point where steam was blasting out of my ears by the time the lecture ended, and I erupted at a nearby diner.

"How dare they stand on that stage and take credit for their gift, as if God had nothing to do with it? And how dare they treat it as if it has no more significance than a parlor game and not bother to educate themselves about its potential? A whole audience sitting there looking for answers, looking for comfort about their deceased loved ones, and the whole subject of the spirit surviving death, and all they got back was a bunch of double talk, lies, and half-truths. Not one person in that room learned a damned thing tonight. I certainly didn't. Did you? What a complete waste of an opportunity!"

Dal in particular was just sitting there smiling at me. When I finally paused in mid-tirade to take a breath he said gently, "Can I ask you something?"

"Am I wrong?" I demanded. "Am I being unfair?"

"Not at all. I agree with everything you just said. My question is, what are you going to do about it?"

At that moment, while it might have been Dal's voice, I was hearing my late, great friend Bob Williams as surely as if he were sitting beside me, which he probably was, believing in me, inspiring me to activate my determination "to separate the truth from the nonsense," as he'd put it, and put my spiritual commitment where my mouth was. Thanks to Bob, and Grandma Ada, and Francine, and everyone and everything else that had led me to that moment, I knew exactly what I was going to do about it.

As quickly as a loan for legal expenses and filing the requisite paperwork would allow, I founded the Nirvana Foundation for Psychic Research, registered as a nonprofit organization with the state of California in 1974. It was dedicated to the memory of Bob Williams, and its primary purposes were to teach psychic development and to explore and prove the survival of the spirit after death. I chose the name *Nirvana*, which means "enlightenment," as my prayer for all of us who were involved and/or might be touched by our work along the way—whatever our work turned out to be and wherever it ended up taking us.

I advertised the foundation in the classified ads, and twenty-two people showed up for the first class. It was held in our cozy little townhouse, which accommodated maybe eight people as long as they all inhaled. Those twenty-two people told twenty-two more, who told twenty-two more—sound familiar?—and out of happy necessity we quickly rented the most luxurious office space we could afford: a small waiting room and reception area with an even smaller office for me. I dressed it up with charming curtains to create the illusion that there was a window in what was actually a solid cinderblock wall, and we were officially in business. It felt awkward to me at first to charge for the readings I'd been offering for free for so many years. But for one thing, it was the only way I could afford to make a full-time commitment to the foundation. For another thing, as more and more people had been pointing out to me, making a living putting one's gifts to work is pretty much the definition of virtually every career you can name, so as long as I devoted my gifts to God's greatest good, I had no reason to apologize.

I taught classes in psychic and other extrasensory skills and dream interpretation, a passion of Grandma Ada's that she'd passed along to me. I spoke to countless local organizations. I held gatherings at which I tranced Francine. I became a pro bono consultant for the police department and several medical and psychiatric professionals who I knew would regard me as a last resort when all else failed until I proved myself. Word eventually spread to San Francisco, where I began appearing regularly on a popular show called *People Are Talking*. Before long we needed and were able to afford a larger office, and I hired a handful of enthusiastic employees to answer the constantly ringing phones and increasing stacks of mail. A few of those employees, including a San Jose University student named Larry Beck and his friend Laurie Halseth, also doubled as research assistants, long before computers came along, and Dal became the foundation's full-time business manager.

In an almost "while we're at it" gesture, I decided that it might be a good time to put my master hypnotist certificate to use, and we began adding hypnosis sessions to my schedule of psychic readings, for clients who wanted to quit smoking, lose weight, sharpen their concentration skills, and make any number of other life improvements. I can honestly say that my intention for those sessions, in addition to acting on my strong belief in the potential benefits of hypnosis, was to bring in added income for the Nirvana Foundation for Psychic Research. It never occurred to me that these hypnosis sessions would contribute far more than money to the foundation and its efforts to prove that the spirit survives death.

I was doing hypnotherapy on a new client I'll call Frank who wanted help losing weight. I do my best to maintain a poker face no matter what goes on in my office, but I would still love to have surveillance video of my reaction when, shortly after Frank "went under," he began telling me, in the present tense, about his life in Egypt as a pyramid builder. It was so unremarkable and current to him that you would have thought he'd stopped by to see me on his lunch break and would be heading straight back to put some finishing touches on King Tut's tomb as soon as we were through. After a few minutes of that, and a description of some antigravitational devices he and his crew were using, he slipped into a lengthy, impassioned monologue in what sounded like a steady stream of fluent Martian. It was such a torrent of nonsense syllables, complete with phrasing and even bits of intergalactic humor (judging from his occasional chuckling), that I became convinced he was having a psychotic meltdown right before my eyes. Outwardly I'm sure I appeared calm. Inwardly I was making a mental note to have a panic button installed in my office so that my staff would know to come racing in to save me if I needed them. (I've had a hidden panic button ever since, by the way.) And then, as suddenly as he'd flipped out on me, he snapped right back to the normal, rather shy local tailor who'd walked in forty minutes earlier, with no awareness that anything unusual had happened.

With Frank's permission, I sent a tape of that session to a psychology professor friend at Stanford for his evaluation. If this poor client was in psychiatric trouble, I wasn't qualified to provide it, but I'd move heaven and earth to get him to someone who was, even if I had to drive him there myself.

Three days later my professor friend called, so excited he was sputtering into the phone. "Where the hell did you get this tape?"

I gave a brief, noncommittal explanation, after which he told me that he'd been studying and researching what he heard on that tape and had shared it with colleagues who researched it as well. And they'd come to the unanimous conclusion that the "nonsense syllables" my shy local tailor client had babbled at me were actually a fluent monologue in an obscure seventh-century BC Assyrian dialect that would have been common among pyramid builders.

I was in as much shock as the professor was, to the point where I had no idea what to say. Hard as it may be to believe, I'm one of the most skeptical people you'll ever meet. Maybe it's the Missouri "Show Me" influence, but until I've thoroughly checked something out through research and/or experiencing it for myself, I always look for the logical, "earthly" explanation first. So the first thing I did after hanging up from the professor was call the client and ask him as casually as possible (which wasn't very casually, I'm sure) if by any chance he happened to speak any ancient Assyrian dialects. His response convinced me beyond all doubt that (1) no, he didn't, and (2) he was as concerned about my sanity by the end of that conversation as I'd been about his.

I have to admit that in all the years of reading and studying I'd done on the subject of reincarnation, I hadn't given it an enormous amount of thought. I didn't believe or disbelieve, although it did seem to answer more questions than it raised, and enough great religions and brilliant minds in a wide variety of fields were convinced enough in the existence of past lives that it was impossible to dismiss it as some goofy fantasy. That hypnosis session didn't convince me, but it threw open a whole new subject for the Nirvana Foundation to investigate.

Regressive hypnosis wasn't new to me. I'd found a lot of value in taking people back to their birth in this lifetime, where very often along the way we'd find the key to the problem they'd come to me to solve. So regressing people to lifetimes before this one wasn't a huge stretch. It was just a matter of breaking through my own self-imposed boundaries and then, as always, making absolutely sure never to lead my clients in any way, letting them lead me through other lives they'd lived. And invariably, they did, client after client, life after life, in amazing detail, all teaching me more than I probably ever taught them and all having a couple of things in common:

Every single client described exactly the same experience as they made the transition from one past life to the next, no matter how or where they died: the tunnel; the brilliant white Light of pure, peaceful love and wisdom at its end; moving through the Light to an impossibly beautiful meadow where their deceased loved ones (including their beloved animals) were waiting to welcome them Home; and a view of magnificent buildings that they recognized as the entrance to the Other Side.

And, without exception, not one client was ever traumatized by telling me about a past-life death, but each and every one of them went through a nightmarish ordeal as they relived their birth into this life. I caught on very quickly that putting them through their memories of being born wasn't worth the effort, and that we all waste a lot of emotional energy fearing death when we've already been through something much scarier. Let's put it this way: at the end of our current lives waits a vast, glittering tunnel that leads us to the most sacred, wondrous white Light we'll ever see and on to a reunion with everyone we've ever loved who left this earth. At the beginning was a cramped dark tunnel called a birth canal, through which we were squooshed until we plopped into the Latex-gloved hands of a bunch of strangers under the harsh white glare of a fluorescent ceiling fixture. All things considered, which of those sounds more worth fearing to you?

Several of my friends in the psychiatric and medical fields were also researching reincarnation at the time, and rarely did a day go by when we weren't consulting with each other about our latest questions, progress, and theories. One of us came up with the idea of holding a public panel discussion on the general subject of past lives and the work we'd been doing, and a standing room–only crowd assembled in a huge auditorium in San Jose to hear what we had to say. I'll be the first to admit that I felt outclassed on that panel and suggested we bill ourselves as "Five Renowned, Big-Deal Doctors . . . and Sylvia." I tried to make up the difference by offering to do a live past-life regression onstage, on a random audience volunteer. My colleagues were a little hesitant at first—what if, while hundreds of people looked on, the volunteer turned out to be a resistant hypnosis subject, or one of those rare people who was experiencing their first lifetime on earth and just sat silently onstage for half an hour like a bucket of rocks? My argument: On the other hand, what if it works? And how will we know one way or the other if we don't try? I won.

Out of a handful of volunteers, I chose a conservative-looking young man I'll call Tom, who'd been respectful enough to wear a suit and tie to the event but seemed to be torn between buying into this reincarnation idea and walking out of the auditorium laughing himself senseless. As I did with every client in my office, I asked before hypnotizing Tom if he had any persistent physical or emotional problems he'd like to address, or any phobias that were getting in his way. He revealed that he had a chronically painful right foot that continued to mystify any number of podiatrists, and that for as long as he could remember he'd harbored a secret fear that no matter how hard he tried or how successful he became, those around him would always see through the façade and recognize how inadequate and undeserving he really was.

Like most open-minded skeptics, he was a good subject to work with, cooperative but insistent on authenticity, leaving no doubt that he wasn't "under" until he was genuinely *under*. I was slow and methodical about regressing him to demonstrate the process for the audience and to leave no doubt that I wasn't leading him, that every bit of information was coming from him, not from me.

We worked our way back through this lifetime, past his birth, past the moment of his conception, and arrived at his death in a life before this one. And then, with no warning and no cue from me of any kind, we all watched with fascination as Tom's demeanor subtly but decidedly changed. His self-confident posture slumped a bit as if he were shrinking into a sad, apologetic shell, and his right foot seemed to shrivel and turn in as if it were deformed.

"What is today's date?" I asked him.

He gave me a specific date in 1821.

"What is your name?"

It was a male name that bore no resemblance to the one with which he'd introduced himself to us that day.

"And where are you?"

He said he was at his family's farmhouse on the outskirts of a small town in Virginia and went on to describe a brief, sad lifetime. He was the youngest of six children, but unlike his five siblings, he was born with a clubbed right foot. As a result, through no fault of his own, he was more of a disappointing burden than a help to his family on their modest farm, and although he was a hard-working student who excelled at school and tried his best to make friends, he couldn't overcome being a lonely object of ridicule among his classmates. He died of pneumonia at the age of fifteen and beamed with joy as he described the sacred peace of going Home again, where everyone was cherished equally as God's beloved children.

There wasn't a dry eye in the house as I brought him back to the present again, and on an impulse, before I "woke him up," I gave him a posthypnotic suggestion that I've used in every regressive hypnosis session since:

> When you open your eyes, you'll embrace all the joy and wisdom of every life you've ever lived, while all the pain and sorrow from those lives will be resolved forever in the sacred peace of the white Light of the Holy Spirit.

Tom's posture was straight and sure again and his right foot looked completely normal as he left the stage with no memory of how he'd spent the previous thirty minutes. He reported several months later that he hadn't suffered another moment of pain in his right foot, and his private fear of being inadequate and undeserving of his success had "somehow" been replaced by a refreshing sense of self-confidence.

I think part of my earlier disinterest in past lives came from my inability to understand their relevance in the lifetimes we're living now. Discovering that I'd once been the most beautiful high priestess in all of Africa and that in a later life I'd been the first Eskimo to use shoelaces might make for interesting cocktail party conversation, but in the big picture, so what, and what possible good would it do me to know that? After the weight loss hypnosis session with the pyramid builder, I got around to asking Francine what the point was of unearthing previous incarnations and pursuing regressive hypnosis. Her answer was a simple, "Healing." I had no idea what she meant until that experience with Tom on an auditorium stage, and from that day on I promised myself, Francine, and all the regressive hypnosis clients still to come that I would do everything in my power, with God's help, to access the healing that was buried in their spirits' memories.

There was one minor obstacle, which became apparent as I began doing more and more regressions. Most clients wanting regressive hypnosis are either consciously or subconsciously looking for help with a medical or psychological problem that traditional treatment hasn't solved. (And if you don't already know this about me, I want to clarify it now: I'm a huge fan of medical and psychiatric professionals, and I'll *always* advocate that you turn to them first. *Never* use me or any other psychic as a substitute for licensed, qualified care. At our best, we can serve as worthwhile complements, nothing more.) But once those clients start experiencing their past lives and the sheer fascination of remembering them, they turn into five-year-olds on their first trip to Disneyland. They can spend hours, literally, rooting around in their spirits' history, so that finding the core of their current problem gets lost in all the "new" information.

I complained to Francine about this inefficient aspect of regressive hypnosis, and she gave me the solution: "Tell your clients to go to the 'point of entry.'"

I know. I didn't know what that meant either. But it made all the sense in the world to my clients while they were under. The point of entry is essentially the specific event in the specific past life that's causing some kind of pain or obstacle in this life. Uncovering it is like removing a long-buried thorn so that healing can begin. I have no idea why it works, but it does—telling a client to go to the point of entry while they're frolicking through irrelevant incarnations is like hitting a fast-forward button. They race to the lifetime, and the situation in that lifetime, where the thorn is hidden, and once they discover it and exorcise it by talking about it, the wound heals.

The foundation was flooded with requests for regressive hypnosis in addition to psychic readings, classes, lectures, channeling sessions, talk show appearances, and other pursuits we were exploring (more about those in other chapters), and it became apparent that I needed help to manage it all. I couldn't teach my staff to become psychics. (That's the reason to avoid psychic hotlines, by the way—those aren't actual psychics you're talking to, they're trained telemarketers who are skilled in the art of the "cold reading," a script that can trick you into not noticing that all the information you're hearing is actually coming from you.) But I could train them to become legitimate regressive hypnotists. I gave crash courses to those on my staff who were interested and talented at it, with the added bonus of the point of entry tip, and the foundation's files on survival of the spirit began to fill every available square inch of our offices, thanks in part to the sessions my staff took over on my behalf.

There was one more time-consuming but essential aspect of past-life regressions that had to be dealt with: the Nirvana Foundation needed to establish credibility with the regressions it conducted to separate real past lives from the false memories that are common in hypnosis. If a client experienced a previous incarnation as, let's say, a third-generation beekeeper named Robert Shoup who died in Bunyonville, Minnesota, in 1810, we went as far as our pre-computer, pre-Google research could take us, usually through the amazing San Bruno Archives, to establish that yes, there really was such a place as Bunyonville, Minnesota, in the early 1800s, and yes, a beekeeper named Robert Shoup died there in 1810. It was tedious work but worth every minute—it never ceased to amaze us how many of those past lives we were able to confirm, and we still have every one of those session files today. (Thank you, God, for the interim invention of storage units.)

Not all of my past-life work involved formal hypnosis sessions, incidentally. One day, purely out of curiosity, I casually asked Chris, who was four years old at the time, "Who were you before this?" He answered just as casually that he was a cowboy, with a horse named Cinnamon, and he died in the street in front of a place with two swinging doors (probably a saloon) from a gunshot in the stomach. A woman held his head in her lap while he died. What do you think, was it a coincidence that Chris's chronic stomach problems in this life vanished after that brief conversation?

Eventually Francine explained these physical manifestations of past-life events as something called "cell memory." I've written books about it and the countless examples of it I've come across, so I'm not about to belabor it here, but what it boils down to is that our spirits enter our bodies with memories of all our past lives completely intact. Our spirits keep those memories alive and well in our subconscious minds, and the cells of our bodies are programmed to react literally to the information they receive from the subconscious, including our spirits' memories, with no way to discern past, present, or future. So by accessing those cell memories, we can rid ourselves of long-buried physical, mental, and emotional obstacles.

Cell memory also explains those experiences many of us have had in which we travel to a place we've never been before (in this lifetime) and find it to be eerily familiar. We know our way around, we know about buildings that verifiably used to exist there, we know what we'll find around the next bend and over the next hill, and all "for no apparent reason" (that wonderful euphemism the scientific community often uses for "Beats me"). There *is* an apparent reason: cell memory. To be fair, I didn't make that connection until Dal and I began traveling extensively and I had my share of firsthand encounters with what's called "morphic resonance"—cell memory applied to the location of a past life, so deeply and profoundly that the whole body, even the conscious mind, resonates with the familiarity of it.

But extensive traveling was still a few years away. For the time being, I was almost too busy to manage a trip to the bathroom. I was a very involved mother, a wife, a daughter, a homemaker, a psychic, a hypnotist, a lecturer, a trance medium (the proper term for someone who channels spirits, as I was doing regularly with Francine), a television talk show guest, a researcher, a teacher at weekly foundation classes—in other words, a woman who was burning herself out and never saw it coming.

AS SOMETIMES HAPPENS when I'm overwhelmed, I began sinking into a deep depression.

Since I know that's not uncommon, it's worth mentioning that I later learned to call it a "psychic attack." Please don't let that conjure up an image of me on a rampage through Cleveland with a machine gun. The term refers to an attack on the psyche when we involuntarily begin hearing and believing all the negative, debilitating, confidence-shattering "tapes" that play over and over and over again in our minds when we're exhausted, ill, and/or far too busy for our own good. The tapes are the insults and insulting thoughts aimed at us by the dark entities we've let into our lives. The more you talk to your friends and loved ones, the more you discover that all of our tapes sound horribly similar:

Nothing I've ever done or ever will do really matters. I've been kidding myself thinking I'm accomplishing anything worthwhile, or that I could ever make a difference in anyone's life. I could never get out of bed again and nobody's world would be diminished one bit except that they'd have to wash their own dishes and do their own laundry, and they'd probably do a better job of it anyway. . . .

At the same time I learned about psychic attacks I learned (a) that they're exactly the reason we need to go as far out of our way as possible to avoid dark entities and the negativity they spread, and (b) to remind ourselves that these demeaning thoughts aren't facts, they're implanted tapes of insults we don't deserve. It helps to reach up to that spot between and slightly above our eyes (where our third eye would be) and give a little push with the forefinger, as if we're ejecting those awful tapes from our heads. While I do that I always say, for added reinforcement, "I refuse this tape and all other tricks of the dark entities around me, and I release their negativity from my mind to be resolved forever into the white Light of the Holy Spirit."

Don't believe me? Try it anyway. It's harmless, it takes about two seconds, and it beats resigning yourself to being depressed and miserable and doing nothing about it at all.

Back then, though, before I knew about psychic attacks, I was depressed and miserable and doing nothing about it at all except trying to make myself even busier to avoid dealing with it. Predictably, I got so busy that I was just blasting through life at hyperspeed, not paying attention, and promptly broke my foot while flying down a flight of stairs.

Then, because our state of mind *always* reflects itself in our physical health for better or worse, as soon as my foot healed, it was off to the hospital for what we'll politely call an "unanticipated" hysterectomy.

And take it from me, nothing says "Slow down!" like flatlining after surgery and having the profound honor of your very own near-death experience.

The problem was the IV drip of Demerol that I'd been given to help control postoperative pain. I guess someone forgot to make a note on my chart that I'm violently allergic to Demerol. (In fact, I'm violently allergic to anything stronger than one Excedrin.) My family and close friends were keeping a round-the-clock vigil beside my hospital bed when suddenly my body temperature and blood pressure plummeted and my heart stopped.

I've talked to a lot of people who've had near-death experiences, and most of them have distinct memories of hovering above their hospital beds or operating tables, fascinated by the realization that they're observing their own lifeless bodies from an aerial view and hearing every word being said around them. I apparently couldn't wait to head Home, because I didn't stick around to hover—I went straight into the legendary tunnel.

As I mentioned earlier, Francine had assured me and hundreds of lecture audience members that the Other Side exists just three feet above the earth's surface. That made all the sense in the world to me when I saw that, rather than descending from some distant galaxy, the tunnel rose from the etheric substance of my body, not leading up but leading across at about a thirty-degree angle. I have no memory of exactly how I entered the tunnel, but I remember with crystal clarity the thrilling, weightless freedom of traveling through it. I felt more alive, more peaceful, and more joyful than at any moment in the lifetime I was leaving behind. There was no conscious worry about everyone on earth I loved; I just knew I'd be visiting them soon from Home and that we would be together again in what would seem like an instant, since there is no such thing as time on the Other Side. There was no conscious thought of God's promise of eternity; I was just filled with the sacred, familiar certainty of it. There was no conscious thought of fear or sorrow; I just knew I was on my way Home to resume my perfect, stimulating life there, armed with the newly acquired lessons I'd learned in this latest incarnation. There was no conscious thought of the flawed, struggling, finite body I'd left behind. I just knew I felt like a butterfly must feel when it emerges so exquisitely beautiful from the confines of its cocoon.

The Light appeared ahead of me. It defies worldly description—there's simply nothing on this plane to compare it to. It's a pure, brilliant, all-encompassing white, and somehow it seems to contain all the love, peace, wisdom, and sanctity that ever existed and that ever will exist.

A figure stepped into the tunnel ahead of me, an unrecognizable silhouette at first against the white sun of Light. But as I moved closer the features became clear. It was Grandma Ada, beaming at me, loving me immeasurably, and I silently called out to her, rushing toward her to feel her arms around me again. There was a meadow beyond her, a blanket of green grass and flowers whose colors were enriched and magnified by a thousand beyond anything on earth.

Then two things happened simultaneously:

Almost to Grandma Ada, I reached out to touch her, and when I was just a breath away, she extended her hand toward me, her palm facing me, wordlessly telling me to stop. . . . At that same instant I clearly heard, from a great distance away, the voice of one of the friends I'd left standing beside my hospital bed, urgently pleading, "Sylvia, don't go, you're so needed!"

It was exactly as if a giant rubber band had been wrapped around my waist and stretched to its limit. I felt myself being snapped from that tunnel Home, that Light, that stunning meadow, and the touch of my grandma's hand, and I slammed back into the sick, painful, leaden body lying on that sterile bed in that sterile hospital room, gazing into the weeping, grief-stricken faces staring at me.

I tried to be grateful that I was back—obviously there was more work for me to do here, and I'm no quitter. But it took time for me to stop yearning for the heaven, the reunions, the bliss, and the *real* life that had literally been almost within my reach.

In all these years since, I've come to cherish that exquisite event. I've read about and heard countless near-death experiences from authors, clients, friends, and colleagues from every walk of life, every circumstance, every faith, and almost every continent on earth. I deeply appreciate that I was given the opportunity to stop listening as a researcher and regressive hypnotist and to start listening as someone who can say, and mean, "I know. I've been there too."

It's a real source of fascination to me, by the way, that many "experts" and closed-minded skeptics attribute near-death experiences to hallucinations caused by the brain being deprived of oxygen. And yet, the tens or hundreds of thousands of strangers from all over the world who've described our near-death experiences seem to have exactly the same oxygen-deprived hallucinations.

How's that for an unbelievable coincidence?

And I do mean "unbelievable."

It was while I was recovering that Francine explained something called "exit points." It seems that when we write our charts, we include five exit points, or five different ways and means to get ourselves Home again. They're circumstances we devise that can end these incarnations if and when we choose to take advantage of them. We don't necessarily space them out evenly over the course of our lifetime—we might create two exit points in the first three years, for example, then another one or two in our fifties and our fifth one on our hundredth birthday. Nor do we necessarily wait until our fifth exit point to decide that we've accomplished what we came here for. Instead, we can leave on any one of the five. The "terminal" illnesses from which people "impossibly" recover? Exit points they chose not to take. Minor car accidents in which there's an "inexplicable" fatality? An exit point the fatality decided to cash in. My near-death experience? As Francine pointed out, it wasn't really Grandma Ada's choice after all, or the choice of the friend who begged me not to leave that brought me back. It was God's choice and mine, as intensely personal a decision as any of us will ever make. Next time a loved one goes Home despite all your prayers for them to stay, don't believe for one second that your prayers weren't answered. For their own reasons, your loved one simply took advantage of one of their exit points, and someday the two of you will have an eternity to talk about it.

————

OBVIOUSLY THE END of that story is that I rejected that exit point. I healed, physically and emotionally, very aware that I must have come back for some very good reasons. Thanks to my family and the increasing scope of the Nirvana Foundation, I didn't have to look any farther than my heart and soul to discover what those reasons were.

FOUR

GHOST STORIES

As soon as word got around that there was such a thing as a foundation dedicated to psychic research, our office was inundated with calls asking me to find, identify, and usually get rid of alleged ghosts. Ghosts, after all, are more proof of the survival of the spirit after death, which was one of the Nirvana Foundation's stated goals, so I was happy to oblige. Besides, ghosts are fascinating, tragic, and invariably in need of help finding their way Home, and the least I could do was try.

I saw my first ghost when I was nine years old. Daddy had moved us to a beautiful seventy-five-year-old Queen Anne-style house on Charlotte Street in Kansas City that included an attic, a basement, a butler's pantry, and, best of all, bedrooms for Grandma Ada and Brother, who moved there with us.

One Saturday a few weeks after we settled in I came out of my bedroom to discover an elderly man with a full head of white hair and a white beard, wearing a handsome uniform draped with gold military braids, standing in the hallway. He wasn't distinct enough to be earthly, but he was more distinct than any spirit I'd ever seen, and I stared at him and smiled, fascinated by him. He seemed pleased that I could see him and smiled back. His voice wasn't nearly as high pitched as Francine's spirit voice as he uttered the single word, "Basement."

I had no idea what that meant, but at nine years old, I didn't care. If there was a secret or a mystery of some kind in the basement, I was determined to find it, and I raced down the stairs to begin searching. It didn't take long to notice a smooth rock that didn't quite fit in the middle of a wall of otherwise rough-hewn stones. I found a small pickax in a pile of rusted tools, took a strong swing at the smooth rock and easily punctured it, revealing a hollow space behind it. I reached into the space and immediately felt a thick bundle of paper. A pile of money, I thought! What else could it possibly be? I was rich! I'm sure I was already trying to decide what to buy first when I pulled it out to start counting it.

I was crestfallen to discover that my ticket to unimaginable wealth was nothing but a stack of worthless folded-up papers, all but one of which disintegrated into dust in my hand. The one fragile document that stayed in one piece was a handwritten essay, faded and barely readable except for the bold, flowing signature of its author, Captain Frederick Bonneville.

I raced back upstairs to find Grandma Ada, show her my discovery, and tell her about the uniformed gentleman with the white beard who'd directed me to it. That was the day I got my first lesson about ghosts from both Grandma Ada and Francine—poor lonely souls, trapped between the dimensions of earth and the Other Side, not having the slightest idea that they're dead, and wondering who all these intruders are who keep invading their space without even the common decency to acknowledge their existence.

We learned from some elderly neighbors, by the way, that our house was built and loved by a sea captain named Frederick Bonneville. They showed us some grainy group photos from a few Charlotte Street gatherings, and I instantly pointed out the much younger but unmistakable captain who'd greeted me in the hallway and introduced me to that sad, confused world where ghosts live, waiting to go Home.

It's easier than you might think to tell the difference between ghosts and spirits, for perfectly logical reasons. Ghosts are clearer and more distinct to us humans than spirits are, because they haven't transcended to the higher frequency of the Other Side yet. Ghosts move among us at our ground level, while spirits seem to float—in reality, spirits don't float at all, they're simply moving at *their* ground level, three feet above ours. Spirits have experienced the healing and bliss of Home and will always appear healed, healthy, and happy, but ghosts still bear signs of any injuries, illness, deformities, confusion, anger, and other earthly challenges they struggled with during their lifetime. Even those ghosts who seem perfectly pleasant, like Captain Bonneville, don't belong here, not because they mean us harm but because they're spirits who are denying themselves their rightful, peaceful joy in God's arms.

A very common attitude about hauntings is summed up in this quote from the prolific author Anonymous: "I've never believed in ghosts, but I've been afraid of them all my life." So it was no surprise that call after call after call to the foundation asking me to provide ghost-busting services started with the words, "I know this sounds ridiculous, but. . . ."

The protocol for every haunting investigation was that I always took a team of my research staff with me, not out of fear but for verification purposes, and there was always at least a tape recorder if not a whole battery of devices to memorialize the experience. No research was ever done beforehand, so that I would never walk in with any predisposed opinions, but thorough research was done after the fact to verify whatever information came through.

And it's worth noting that in more than half of the investigations we did on "things that go bump in the night," my conclusion was that the people involved didn't need me, they needed an exterminator to get rid of the critters in their attic and/or a chainsaw to cut down the tree limb that was brushing against their window and scaring them during the night. It became a source of fascination for me that these people who called the foundation because they were so terrified of being haunted were usually more disappointed than relieved when I broke the news that they were completely ghost-free.

I've successfully sent a few ghosts into the tunnel to the Light, which, to oversimplify it only a little, boils down to a compassionate but firm, "You're dead. Go Home." It doesn't always work—it depends on the reasons they've stayed behind (and they always have a reason) and how determined they are to stick around. But Francine assures me that sooner or later the spirit world comes to retrieve those ghosts who refuse to leave and delivers them safely to the Other Side.

Starting in the late 1970s, I investigated more hauntings than I can count, some of them more famous and memorable than others. As I said earlier, each of them, in their own way, was too fascinating and too sad to forget.

THE SLAUGHTER HOUSE

I know. You live in a house with the unfortunate nickname "The Slaughter House" and it surprises you that something's bothering you about it? When I got a call asking me to check out a reported haunting at the modest home in the San Francisco Bay Area and heard that the couple who lived there was being terrorized by an entity of some kind, I asked the obvious question, "Why don't they move?" The answer was, "They can't afford it." For obvious reasons, I had no trouble relating to that.

While I never do preliminary research on a haunting, I admit it, I couldn't resist asking where on earth the name "The Slaughter House" came from. The caller couldn't have been more vague— there were rumors about a murder in the house, or maybe a double homicide, or rumors of a double homicide, several owners ago, or renters, or somebody who lived there, they weren't sure. I listened to a good minute of stammering, sorry that I'd brought it up and idly wondering why some people have such an aversion to the simple phrase, "I don't know." In the end, I thanked the caller for the (lack of) information and scheduled a trip to the house.

From the moment my researchers and I arrived, it was obvious that the owners of the Slaughter House, whom I'll call Greg and Joan, were genuinely frightened and were very serious about getting to the bottom of what was going on in their home—I was barely out of the car when a busy swarm of ghost-busting technicians they'd hired began draping me with infrared cameras, heat sensors, and other state-of-the-art (at the time) recording equipment.

Greg and Joan and I gathered in the living room, where they described what they'd been going through since almost their first night in the house. There were unexplainable footsteps, slamming doors in unoccupied parts of the house, glimpses of grotesque faces at the windows, and the cold spots that very often signal the presence of a ghost. It's worth mentioning that Greg and Joan were lovely, "normal" people who had no interest in notoriety; they just wanted a house to live in that didn't scare them senseless.

And, assuming they were being truthful about the worst of what they'd gone through, I would have been scared too, and I don't scare easily. On more than one occasion they'd both awakened during the night to find a man standing over their bed, staring at them in wild, insane outrage. They had the sense that the source of his wrath had to do with finding the two of them in bed together.

"He even grabbed my arm one night," Joan said with tears in her eyes. "His hand was amazingly strong and ice cold, and the feel of him touching my skin was repulsive."

"I saw it happen, and I couldn't do a damned thing about it. By the time I jumped out of bed to go after him, he'd vanished," Greg added. It was the sad confession of a man who still hadn't forgiven himself for not being able to protect his wife, and I assured him there was nothing he or anyone else would have done any differently in that situation.

These were nice people. I wanted very much to help them. The problem was, I hadn't sensed a single thing wrong in that house so far, nor had my thousand or so added pounds of equipment. I excused myself and headed into the kitchen. Nothing. I stepped into the small dining room. Still nothing. Then I proceeded down the narrow hallway toward the bedrooms and walked into a cold spot. I never saw it or sensed it coming, I just found myself in the middle of a small, isolated area so cold that it went straight through to my bones, and I could see my breath in an un-air-conditioned house in July. One of the technicians who was monitoring the equipment came racing out of a nearby room to pull me back, I guess because the machines had suddenly gone crazy. I waved him away with a silent signal that I was okay and kept moving through the cold spot and on to the master bedroom.

Every haunting has a "heart," a core from which all its energy emanates. In the Slaughter House, the heart of the haunting was the master bedroom. The air in that room felt thick and highly charged, the feeling of a force field that makes the hair stand up on the back of your neck. My heart was pounding as I sat down on the bed, and my adrenalin was pumping with the growing awareness that I was being watched by someone unearthly.

He was staring in at me from a window beside the bed, a broad, handsome man with thick dark hair. I met his eyes and stared back, refusing to look away to establish that, yes, I could see him, and no, I wasn't going to run screaming from the room. He didn't have that much power over me.

I said, "Come in," and an instant later he was standing in front of me, holding a scythe. It was clearly old and had a wooden handle and a long serrated crescent blade. I refused to react; I just kept my focus on his eyes. It seemed to intrigue him, and after a long silence he gave a small nod and said, "My name is Giovanni. And yours?"

I introduced myself and then asked him why he was there.

"I'm sad because my wife is gone," he told me quietly.

I was psychically flooded with images. This same room. A different bed. A man asleep, resembling Giovanni but definitely not him. A dark-haired woman sleeping beside him. Giovanni, his face tear-stained, moving silently toward the bed, the scythe raised above his head.

"Giovanni, did you kill someone?"

He began to weep as the story spilled out of him. "It was wrong what my brother did. I brought Maria here from Italy to be my wife, and while I worked in the hot fields they were here betraying me, making love in our bed. I made them both sorry that they did this to me."

I kept all judgment and emotion out of my voice to keep him talking. "After you killed them, what did you do next?"

"I ran away," he said. "I hid in the hills for a long time. Then I became very sick, and that's the last thing I remember."

Translation: With nothing but the bloody clothes he was wearing, he disappeared into the cold, damp hills near the bay and died of pneumonia without realizing it. I explained that to him, assuring him that he didn't have to be trapped here on earth any more, that it was time for him to go toward the Light now, where he would find peace.

He shook his head. "I can't face God. He'll never forgive me."

"Giovanni, I don't know anything about a God who doesn't forgive. The God I know is all loving, all knowing, all forgiving, and embraces every one of us who holds out our arms to Him, I promise you."

We talked for nearly two hours, and he knew I was telling him the truth. At best, he would join his wife and brother at Home and learn that they forgave him many decades ago, and that God never stopped loving him unconditionally. At worst, he would come right back to earth to be born again and given another lifetime to make amends for the lives he took. Either way, it would be a step forward, toward hope and freedom from this terrible, hopeless hell of guilt in which he was trapped.

He finally agreed to go. I gave him one more nod of encouragement and reassurance. He simply said, "You'd better be right," and he disappeared.

There was one more memorable moment from that unforgettable day. I was walking to the car, exhausted, when one of my staff asked, "What's that on your arm?" I looked at my upper right arm and saw a perfect equilateral triangle etched into my skin, the exact sign of the Holy Trinity—the Father, the Son, and the Holy Spirit.

Never before or since have I been marked in any way during a haunting. I've investigated hauntings in which people claimed to have been seriously wounded by ghosts, but somehow, every single time, the injuries had healed by the time I got there, sometimes within a few short hours. (Amazing, huh?) There was no mark on my arm before I entered the house. At no time did Giovanni touch me, and I know I didn't give in to a spontaneous whim to scratch an equilateral triangle into my arm. Six of us saw it there, and six of us saw it disappear. I still have no idea what it was. Even Francine has never commented on it.

By all accounts, though, including letters and phone calls from Greg and Joan, there was peace in the Slaughter House from that day on, and it was never disturbed by an earthbound spirit again.

ALCATRAZ

In 1984, many years after the infamous island prison in the San Francisco Bay had closed its doors to inmates, a CBS news crew accompanied me to Alcatraz. A night ranger there had reported what he described as "odd disturbances." He and a former inmate named Leon Thompson accompanied me, my staff, and the news crew into that doomed, hollow place.

One of our first stops on the tour was the prison hospital. I was drawn like a magnet to one of the cells there and couldn't take my eyes off of it as I walked to it—I psychically saw the letter *S* on its bars, and notes, cards, drawings, and other scraps of paper covering every square inch of its bare block walls. Everyone had been instructed not to tell me a single detail about the prison until and unless I asked, so only after I'd focused on that cell and reported what I'd seen inside it did the night ranger explain that for more than ten years it housed Robert Stroud, the famous "Birdman of Alcatraz." Stroud hadn't been allowed to share a cell with live birds since his transfer from Leaven-worth, where he'd become a respected and even published researcher on bird diseases and cures. Instead, he covered the walls of his Alca-traz prison hospital cell with bird-related notes, cards, and drawings, all of them long gone after his death from natural causes in 1963.

The only ghost I saw at Alcatraz appeared in the prison laundry room. He was tall and bald, with small, untrusting eyes. I got the initial *M*, but he told me telepathically (silently, directly from his mind to mine) that he was known as Butcher. Former prisoner Leon Thompson remembered an inmate called "The Butcher," a convicted mob hit man named Abie Maldowitz, who was killed by another prisoner in the laundry room where we were standing.

Abie was walking toward me, staring at me every step of the way. I didn't care at that moment what he'd done during his life-time, I couldn't imagine anything more horrible than the double nightmare of being an earthbound soul in this of all places, and I started telling him, calmly and compassionately, that he was dead, that he didn't have to be a prisoner for one more minute, and that he was free to go Home now, where so many loved ones were waiting to welcome him.

He kept right on coming, closer and closer, his face never changing expression. It couldn't have been more apparent that he wasn't about to listen to a word I had to say, no matter how long I kept talking or how much I meant it. There was nothing he hadn't heard during his lifetime, and trusting people had never paid off. Add to that the desperate confusion of not knowing his life had ended, and I could see it was time to step aside and let Francine take her best shot with him.

We held an impromptu séance. I heard the recording later. Francine's first words to Abie were, "Don't be afraid. We're not here to hurt you." She went on to tell him that she knew all about his life and how he'd ended up at Alcatraz and that profound peace and forgiveness were waiting for him on the Other Side. "When I leave Sylvia's body, I'll be returning there," she said. "Please come with me. There are people there who care about you and want to help you."

After a long silence he replied with what was probably the one safe position his painful lifetime had taught him to take: "I don't believe you."

Abie "The Butcher" Maldowitz is still a prisoner of his own deep anguish at Alcatraz, and there are still any number of strange disturbances on the prison grounds that have now become a state park. Unlike true dark entities, his remorse over the crimes he committed is genuine, and Francine assures me that he will be welcomed at Home with open arms, so please remember him in your prayers, as I do in mine to this day.

THE WINCHESTER MYSTERY HOUSE

The Winchester Mystery House is a legendary monstrosity of a mansion in San Jose, and when a Los Angeles television show called *Evening Magazine* asked me to check out the countless ghost sightings there, I leapt at the invitation.

The story goes that in 1884 Sarah Winchester, heiress to the Winchester weapons fortune and clearly possessed of more money than practicality, began building the mansion as a collaborative effort between her and a committee of spirits from whom she received messages every night in her blue séance room. If I sound a little skeptical about that, it's only because I am. It seems that Sarah had been told by a local medium that a terrible curse had been placed on her by all the vengeful souls who'd died on the wrong end of a Winchester firearm, and her only hope of escaping the curse was to build a house so complex that those vengeful souls couldn't find her. So rather than telling her the truth—that there is no such thing as curses, with the exception of self-inflicted ones brought on by *believing* you've been cursed—her team of spirit architects participated in this nonsense and coached her through the construction of a house that can only be described as just plain incomprehensible.

Estimates indicate that in the course of this construction, as many as 750 rooms were built, destroyed, redesigned, rebuilt, relocated, and redestroyed. Sarah, on leaving the blue séance room every evening after that night's spirit consultation, slept in a different bedroom in a different wing of the house, in keeping with her cunning curse escape plan. She was completely reclusive except for the endless stream of contractors and their crews and a battery of caretakers and staff. She was never more than a few steps away from a maze of secret passageways, trap doors, and other hiding places. And in the end, sure enough, she died. In her sleep, in 1922. At the age of eighty-five. After a lifetime of running from a curse whose only power was her belief in it.

When the building frenzy finally stopped with Sarah's death, the Winchester Mystery House that stood and still stands today numbered 160 rooms, a labyrinth of endless hallways, some of which end in closets or solid walls or even the back of a walk-in freezer. Having heard that spirits enjoy traveling through chimneys and wanting to encourage their presence, Sarah saw to it that forty-seven chimneys were placed throughout the house. As an homage to the number with which she was most obsessed, she ordered thirteen cupolas on the greenhouse roof, thirteen palms to line the driveway, thirteen drainage holes in the kitchen sink, thirteen lights in the chandeliers, and ceilings composed of thirteen panels. There was once a wine cellar in which Sarah became convinced that she'd seen the handprint of the devil, and she had the room sealed and encased with walls so securely that it's still never been found.

I'd already been to the Winchester Mystery House a few times when the television crew asked to film me there. There was no way the Nirvana Foundation was going to ignore exploring a local landmark that was rumored to have been designed during nightly séances to ward off a curse from evil spirits. On my first visit, my researchers and I spent the night in one of the parts of the mansion that was never wired for electricity. There were sudden, inexplicable blasts of icy air in rooms with no windows or vents. Two huge fiery red globes of light appeared in midair out of nowhere and then vanished in an instant. We were treated to a busy, colorful light show with no apparent source that flared with spectacular brilliance for a few seconds before disappearing into the darkness. Throughout the night we heard hammering on metal and wood, footsteps everywhere, doors opening and slamming shut, and the frequent sound of rattling chains, all of which had been consistently reported by a variety of tourists and other visitors. I was surprised that none of my group but me heard the distinct sound of a dirge-like melody playing on an organ, but here's a perfect example of why we never investigated a haunting without a tape recorder that we turned on the moment we stepped onto every property we ever explored and didn't stop until we left: no one else may have heard the organ music but me, but it was perfectly audible on the tape we made that night.

It was also on our first night in the house, when I knew nothing about it except that it was a massive architectural mess and it had been built and owned by an heiress, that I met a ghost couple who introduced themselves as the live-in caretakers. Her name was Susan Hanna, and she wore a white bandanna around her dark hair. His name was Emile Hausen, and he was large and Nordic-looking. Unaware that they were dead and so was Miss Winchester, they'd forfeited their trip Home to stay right where they belonged as far as they were concerned, protecting their beloved employer, her house, and her intense reclusiveness. They weren't threatening to me, but the novelty of having intruders in the house every time they turned around had clearly lost its charm. Sarah Winchester, by the way, was nowhere to be found, and Francine told me she'd gone to the Other Side immediately upon her death.

This was obviously far more than I would prefer to have known ahead of time when I explored the house in the company of the *Evening Magazine* host and crew. I could assure them that the caretaker couple was still in the house, but there was no way I could give the same assurance that we would run into them—ghosts don't exactly come when you call them, after all, and this couple wasn't about to take orders from me or anyone else except Miss Winchester. I wouldn't have minded their refusal to appear so much had it not been for our on-camera host. Talk about an attitude problem. He couldn't have made it clearer that he hadn't enjoyed the six-hour drive from Los Angeles; that he found this assignment to be far beneath his journalistic professionalism; that he no more believed in ghosts than he believed in the tooth fairy; and that he thought I was the goofiest, phoniest waste of time it had ever been his displeasure to interview.

Despite my silent pleas to Susan and Emile to show up just long enough to wipe that condescending smirk off our host's face, they seemed to have taken the day off. Hour after hour went by without a single hint of paranormal activity. The cameras kept rolling, dutifully capturing footage of absolutely nothing, until finally our host had had all he could take of this nonsense. He loudly announced to everyone within earshot, and me in particular, that he was leaving, and he could be contacted outside in the trailer in the snowball's chance in hell that anything remotely interesting seemed to be happening.

He turned to stomp out of the room. As luck would have it, he turned in the direction of the large second-story window we were standing beside. And at that moment, impossible to miss or mistake for anything else, captured on film and in his direct line of vision, the spirit of Sarah Winchester herself floated past the window, a graceful white mist so distinctly ethereal and unexpected that it even startled me before it promptly disappeared before our eyes. Our host wasn't just startled, he froze in place gaping at the window, then turned to me without a drop of blood left in his face, looking exactly like a deer in the headlights. He opted against going outside to the trailer and stayed by my side for the rest of the shoot, as courteous, attentive, and interested as could be. What a relief that I was too much of an adult to say, "Neener." (Okay, I thought it, but I didn't actually say it, so I take the position that it doesn't count.)

Francine tells me that Susan Hanna and Emile Hausen are still diligently working in the Winchester Mystery House, and more than twenty years later I'm still diligently working to validate their existence as employees of Sarah Winchester. A niece of the Winchesters thinks, but isn't sure, that she remembers someone named Emile who worked for the family. That's not enough validation for my taste, or for the Nirvana Foundation, so please do contact my office by phone or e-mail if you have any reliable information to offer.

If nothing else, though, remember them in your prayers along with Abie Maldowitz and all the other ghosts who need our help finding their way Home.

THE BROOKDALE LODGE

The wonderful Henry Winkler was executive producing a television show called *Sightings*, and they asked me to investigate widespread reports of paranormal activity at the Brookdale Lodge, a northern California landmark. No one in Hollywood has a more impeccable reputation than Henry, and the Brookdale Lodge was either famous or infamous, depending on whom you talked to. So the answer was an immediate, "Yes!"

I specifically asked that no one tell me what supposed paranormal activity was going on at Brookdale, but I was given a brief rundown of the lodge's turbulent history. It was built in the late 1800s to be the headquarters of a lumber mill and, in the hundred years since, it had been burned to the ground, abandoned, sold, bought, remodeled, sold again, and remodeled again into the charming restaurant and hotel my staff, the TV crew, and I walked into.

I was glad to see that some of the lodge employees were there when we arrived to either validate or invalidate whatever paranormal information I came up with. I reminded them, and the crew, that it's always a mistake to start any haunting investigation with the assumption that something ghostly is happening. More often than not, floor boards creak because that's what floor boards do when they expand or contract or the building settles. Doors slam shut in a passing breeze with no ghosts or spirits anywhere near them, distant voices are sometimes nothing more than a television or radio left on by mistake, and cold spots are less often ghosts than they are the result of an open window or a need for new insulation in the attic. Not even for the sake of TV cameras would I fake a sighting or expect the employees to validate anything that wasn't true. We were all in agreement to keep our integrity intact throughout the shoot, even if it made for the most boring thirty minutes in television history.

At the employees' suggestion, I started in the dining room, called the Brookroom because of the mountain creek that flows through it—most of the unexplained noises and sightings seemed to emanate from there, they said. So I tuned out all the people and equipment around me and had barely entered the empty room when I heard a child's laughter and looked toward it.

She was adorable, maybe six or seven years old, and she was having a great time running and playing beside the creek while a woman chased her, a part of the game. Suddenly the child scampered toward a small footbridge, lost her footing and slipped, violently hitting her head against the railing with a loud, sickening thud before falling face down into the water. The woman immediately went in after her and collapsed before she reached her.

By definition, ghosts are caught in a time warp—the world around them freezes in place at the moment of their unknowing death, except for the parade of strangers who start intruding in that world for no apparent reason from that moment on. These two ghosts, the child and the woman, were in a variation of that time warp, a nonstop "instant replay" of the sequence of events that ended their lives. As painful as it was to watch, I knew it was decades too late for any rescue efforts I might have to offer, so I turned around to make sure the cameras were rolling. By the time I turned to face the creek again, the little girl was standing in front of me, dripping wet, with a vicious gash in her head that didn't seem to be bothering her in the least.

I smiled at her and asked her if she was all right. She cheerfully nodded, confirming my suspicion that she had no idea she'd just died.

"I'm Sarah," she said, and then pointed to the creek, toward the woman who was still lying motionless in the water. "That's my nanny Maria."

Before I could explain that she and Maria were dead and I could help them go Home, she let out a giggle and scampered away, darting among the dining room tables and chairs and quickly vanishing.

The employees filled me in later: in or around 1950 the lodge owner's niece, a six-year-old named Sarah Logan, drowned in the Brookroom creek, and her nanny died of a heart attack while trying to save her. Apparently countless guests, employees, and lodge owners had been seeing and hearing Sarah for decades, running, playing, and laughing in almost every room at Brookdale, particularly in the dining room where she died. They were grateful for the explanation, and I was grateful for the validation.

The *Sightings* segment director suggested a visit to the ballroom next, another source of rumored strange activity. I heard music before I even got there, so clearly that I was surprised to find out that no one else could hear it but me. It sounded like a live orchestra from the Big Band era, but the vast room and its stage were empty, except for one man, just indistinct enough to be a ghost, staring at me with no expression. He was very stocky, with a moustache, a thick head of hair, and glasses he wore far down on his prominent nose. Other than a few members of the crew who felt a brief cold breeze coming from his direction, I was the only one aware of his presence.

I said hello to him, and he grunted at me.

"I'm Sylvia," I said. "What's your name?"

He didn't like me, and he didn't want me there. It took forever for him to finally mutter the word "judge."

I tried my best to sound friendly and get some kind of conversation rolling. I might as well have been talking to a tree stump. "Your name is Judge? Or you *are* a judge? Or you think I'm here to judge you? I give up, what does 'judge' mean?"

He almost growled the word "judge" again, and then started saying it over and over again as if he were trying to annoy me. If that was his intention, he succeeded beautifully. I'm sympathetic, but I'm also human, and I fleetingly wondered to myself if maybe he died of terminal obnoxiousness. I finally interrupted his nonstop "judge" mantra with one more shot at warming him up.

"I met Sarah and Maria earlier," I offered cheerfully. "Do you know them?"

He gave a resentful none-of-your-business nod and promptly vanished. To this day I have no idea who he was—the employees had never heard of him or anyone fitting that description, and our research turned up nothing. I can't say I miss him. But I did gather the employees, the film crew, and my staff for a prayer circle in the ballroom when we finished filming, asking that the spirits of Sarah, Maria, and yes, even Judge be released into the white Light of the Holy Spirit, to be embraced by God and their loved ones on the Other Side.

I was headed for the door with my staff when I had a once-in-a-lifetime experience—or at least I hope it was once in a lifetime. I happened to glance down at myself and discovered that some kind of thick white sticky substance was smeared across the whole front of my blouse. I'm being polite when I describe it as disgusting. My staff gathered around, not to protect me from the film crew and employees, which would have been a lovely gesture, but to openly gape and point and make "Ewwwww!" and gagging noises. (I love my staff with all my heart, but you have no idea how ornery they can be when they're gathered as a group.)

I couldn't imagine where it came from. I hadn't had anything to eat or drink. And I certainly would have noticed if I'd brushed up against something that had whatever this was all over it. Finally my longtime right-hand man Michael McClellan, kidding but not, suggested, "Don't look now, but I think you've been slimed."

For any of you who missed the movie *Ghostbusters*, "slimed" means being drenched in ectoplasm from an encounter with a ghost. (Ectoplasm is thought to be the tangible residue of cell energy that's transmitted between a spiritual medium and a ghost.) I don't know if that's what it was or not, but I do know that everyone who was with me that day has tried unsuccessfully to come up with any other explanation. I occasionally wish we'd kept a sample of it to have it tested, but in those pre–DNA/pre–*CSI* days it honestly didn't occur to us. (There was also the fact that I threw that disgusting blouse away the minute I got home.) But there you have it, my one and only *possible* slime encounter, and if that's what it was, I appreciate the experience. Once.

THE VINEYARD HOUSE

Leonard Nimoy's series *In Search Of* was the next to call, wanting to televise an investigation of a purportedly haunted restaurant and inn called the Vineyard House in the beautiful rolling hills near Santa Ynez, California. Because of the show's timetable, they gave me more history than I prefer ahead of time, but it sounded like a potentially fascinating experience.

The four-story Vineyard House was built in 1878 by Robert and Louise Chalmers. It was intended to be an elaborate testament to their successful vineyards, their wealth, Robert's political prowess in the California state legislature, and Louise's self-proclaimed expertise in anything and everything involving culture and elegance.

But then, for reasons that have never been clear (although some combination of strokes and dementia might explain it), Robert suddenly suffered a cataclysmic mental breakdown. In response, Louise chained him in the Vineyard House cellar, and he died there three years later.

The Chalmers's vineyards and wealth went straight downhill with the decline of Robert's sanity, and Louise was ultimately left with no choice but to rent out rooms to boarders and to lease out Robert's former quarters in the cellar as a makeshift jail when all the cells were filled in the nearby town of Coloma. She died in 1913, alone and penniless.

After several decades of sporadic, temporary owners and a lot of neglect, the house's potential was recognized by investors who had the patience, respect, and money to restore it to its original handsome dignity, and in 1956 the inn and restaurant known as the Vineyard House opened its doors.

From the moment it became a business, it was plagued by countless reports of employees and guests of a stunning array of bizarre phenomena throughout the mansion. Invisible chains rattled. Skirts rustled. Footsteps echoed up and down the wooden steps. A transparent woman wandered the halls talking quietly to herself. A piano played with no one near it. Doorknobs turned, apparently by their own power. Untouched glasses slid from one end of the bar to the other. Beds unmade themselves in front of gaping witnesses.

A loud drunken group crashed through the front door late one night and stumbled up the stairs, laughing at the top of their lungs. A disgruntled guest, awakened out of a sound sleep, angrily stuck his head out the door of his room to ask them to keep it down and watched in shock as the three offenders slowly disappeared in front of his eyes.

On another memorable night, a terrified couple ran from the inn and called the police to report that they'd heard a murder being committed in the room next to theirs. The police stormed the room minutes later to find it not only peaceful but perfectly intact and completely unoccupied.

I try, I swear I do, to go into every haunting investigation, every reading, every hypnosis session, every aspect of my life with an open mind and as few predispositions as possible. I don't remember when I've struggled with it more than I did in this case. If the ghost of Louise Chalmers did happen to be roaming the halls of the Vineyard House and I did happen to run into her, I wasn't sure how I was going to react. The thought of a woman chaining her mentally ill husband in the basement for three years until he died frankly made steam roll out of my ears. In fact, I was having fantasies of chaining her in the basement for three years to see how *she* liked it, but since you can't really restrain a ghost I knew that wouldn't work. I finally decided that if I couldn't hold my temper with her, I would summon Francine, who can invariably keep a cool, detached head when mine is ready to explode.

Don't you love it when you work up a good case of righteous indignation and then discover you couldn't be more wrong?

There was no doubt about it: both Louise and Robert were still trapped in that house. I caught a glimpse of her in a white chemise watching from an upstairs window when my staff and I arrived, and I felt the two of them there from the moment I stepped in the door. The feeling was that we were all welcome to come and go as we pleased, as long as we understood that we were in their house and they weren't going anywhere no matter how much I blathered about God, a white Light, or some nonsense about their being dead.

What caught me completely off guard was the fact that none of the dark, angry energy I was braced for was anywhere to be found. Somehow, the atmosphere created by the ghosts of Robert and Louise was permeated with great love and kindness. It so threw me, and I'd obviously been so mistaken about what had gone on between them, that I decided to step aside and let Francine take over.

We went to an upstairs bedroom, the room in which I'd seen the woman in white watching us from the window. I remember settling on or beside the brass bed, and I remember the TV cameras, mikes, and lights. I remember my staff being there, as well as some newspaper reporters. But of course from the time I let Francine come in, I don't remember a thing. Although *In Search Of* didn't air what Francine had to say due to time constraints, fortunately the Nirvana Foundation preserved the tapes and the transcripts from that day. Here are some excerpts:

FRANCINE: When Robert's mind became ill . . . [Louise] was
    terribly afraid to have a doctor come in, for fear the doctor

would take him away. She took him to New York, around the turn of the century, to try to get some help for him. They wanted to incarcerate him. She kept saying, over and over again, "He will not be locked in a pesthole." She brought him home, and he had another spell. . . . He fell off his horse and went into a seizure. She and four males took him down to the cellar room with bars on it, to keep him confined and safe, and she tried to give him as much comfort as she possibly could. It was the only way she knew to protect him from being locked away in filthy asylums full of madmen. It was a hard, lonely life for her, but she couldn't bear the thought of him living in chains among strangers who didn't care about him, frightened and abused until his death. It was a tragic story of two people who were very much in love. . . . There is nothing Sylvia or anyone else can do to neutralize this room, or this place. . . . Robert is . . . still in a state of derangement that prevents him from understanding his situation. So he won't go. And if Robert won't go, Louise won't go. It is as simple as that. It is as loving and kind and tragic and simple as that. We're very aware of Robert and Louise on the Other Side . . . and we watch out for them. Someday, in God's wisdom and grace, we will get them and bring them back with us, where they will be healed and happy. Until then, this is where they choose to be . . . and this is where they will stay.

That was more than twenty years ago, and Francine tells me that Robert and Louise are still at Vineyard House, but "it won't be much longer" until they're taken Home. Unfortunately, Francine lives in a place where time doesn't exist and everything is understood in the context of eternity, so "it won't be much longer" could mean decades or even centuries.

I'll always hold that experience especially close to my heart for the reminder I clearly needed, even though I've read it thousands of times in the twenty-six versions of the Bible I've studied and loved: "Judge not, lest ye be judged" (Matt 7:1).

THE MOSS BEACH DISTILLERY

I still get a lot of comments about a haunting I investigated for NBC's *Unsolved Mysteries,* partly because of the show's renewed popularity now that it's available on DVD and partly because of the validation that came afterward.

The Moss Beach Distillery is a cliffside restaurant, twelve miles south of San Francisco, in Half Moon Bay, overlooking the Pacific Ocean. All I was told when my staff and I arrived was that everyone from the owners to the chefs to the waitresses to the customers routinely heard and saw the form of a woman, looking anxious and desperately lost, wandering the dining rooms and the beach below.

It seems that in the late 1920s the Distillery was a popular speakeasy (for you readers who are too young to have a clue what that means, speakeasies were discreet nightclubs where illegal liquor was sold during the Prohibition era). Legend had it that one of the most beautiful and notorious regulars at the Distillery was known as the Woman in Blue, who was rumored to be cheating on her husband with the club's piano player. One night her enraged husband showed up to confront the piano player; the confrontation led to a knife fight on the beach between the two men, and the Woman in Blue was stabbed to death trying to intervene.

The Woman in Blue, like many ghosts, wanted attention. The *Unsolved Mysteries* cameras were rolling when she made herself apparent to me. Sure enough, she was dressed in blue, with a wide-brimmed hat tied with a flowing scarf. Her hairstyle and clothing looked expensive and were undoubtedly very fashionable all those decades ago.

But this poor woman was a tribute to how easily false rumors can blossom into legends that are accepted as fact with no basis in truth whatsoever. She introduced herself to me as Mary Ellen Morley, and she needed my help. She'd been in a terrible car accident, just minutes ago as far as she was concerned, and she was desperately searching for her three-year-old son so that she could comfort him and let him know his mother was okay.

I assured her that all she had to do was follow the Light to the Other Side, where her son who'd died years earlier was waiting for her. She didn't immediately accept the news that she was dead, but she didn't reject it out of hand either—I think it might have cleared up a lot of the confusion she'd been struggling with for so long. Francine tells me that she's safely made it Home now, and that makes me happy no matter who helped her get there.

What I so appreciated about *Unsolved Mysteries* and wish every paranormal-oriented show would make a point of doing today was that their cameras accompanied a couple of the Moss Beach Distillery employees to the local library after my segment had been shot. The employees pored through any number of microfiche records and finally came across the obituary of a woman named Mary Ellen Morley. According to the article, she died in a car accident near the Distillery, and she was survived by her husband and her three-year-old son.

If we pre-computer researchers were able to validate our information before declaring it genuine, there's no earthly excuse for responsible researchers, writers, and producers not to do it now. Let's face it, without validation, even the best ghost story any psychic or medium has to tell is nothing more than fiction.

THE TOYS"R"US GHOST

The ghost I'm asked about most often after years of writing about him can be found to this day at the Toys"R"Us in Sunnyvale, California. His name is Johnny Johnson, and unbeknownst to him, he's been dead since 1884.

I first met him in 1978. Caught in the time warp all ghosts experience, he had no idea he was in a popular toy store. Instead, his reality, then and now, was that he was on the Martin Murphy ranch that existed on that plot of land more than a century ago. He was a young Presbyterian minister who boarded at the ranch and earned his keep as a handyman. His tragedy was that he deeply loved his boss's daughter Beth. Beth was completely unaware of Johnny's feelings for her, and she fell in love with and married another man, who took her home to Boston to start their lives together. Johnny has been hard at work on "the ranch" ever since, truly believing that someday Beth will realize that she loves him too and will come back to be with him where she belongs. His position: If he leaves, how will she be able to find him when she returns from Boston? So there he stays, tending to his vegetable garden by the creek and his other perpetual chores, without a clue that he's actually raking and mulching among aisles of dolls, balls, stuffed animals, and PlayStations.

I took my best shot, several times, at explaining to him that Beth's not coming back, that all he has to do to find her is go toward the Light where she's waiting for him on the Other Side. He wasn't having it and finally got so tired of my incessant blather about it that he snapped, "If you tell me one more time that I'm dead, I'm not going to talk to you any more." He meant it, so to keep the lines of communication open between us I stopped bringing it up.

While Johnny's oblivious to the existence of the store, he's very conscious of its employees and shoppers, most of whom are nothing but annoying intruders as far as he's concerned. He complained to me about it one day, and I think it was the first time the Toys"R"Us manager believed I might not be making up this ghost thing after all.

"Those twin boys who came through here awhile ago were little hellions," Johnny was grumbling under his breath. "Running around, screaming and yelling like wild animals, almost fell in the creek. I've never seen anything like it."

As I left the store that day I asked the manager if he'd happened to notice a pair of twin boys who might have been there earlier.

"Notice them?" he sighed back. "It was impossible not to. Hell on wheels, those two, and their mother just turns them loose and lets them go. She seems to think we're running a day care here or something." Suddenly he stopped and looked at me, curious. "Wait, they left hours ago. How did you know about those boys?"

I smiled and said, "Your ghost told me," and he was a believer from then on.

I went back to the Sunnyvale Toys"R"Us not long ago. I didn't see Johnny Johnson when I first walked in, and I even let myself hope that he'd finally gone Home to reunite with Beth and the other loved ones who were waiting for him.

But I got to the end of a long aisle and there he was, near the back wall of the store. As always, he was limping painfully from the wound in his leg that had killed him more than a hundred years ago, and he was raking invisible leaves by a creek that's long since gone. I asked him how he was, and he just nodded without looking up, too intent on upkeep at the ranch that no longer exists. I left him to his work and walked out.

If you've always wanted to see a ghost but haven't known where one is likely to show up, go to the Sunnyvale, California, Toys"R"Us and keep an eye out for a tall, slender man with a limp, dressed in work clothes, possibly with a straw hat pulled down over his sad, lost eyes to protect him from the sun. Give him a compassionate smile on your way past, and be sure to remember him in your prayers until the spirits on the Other Side come to take him Home to the woman who broke his heart without even knowing.

And in case you're wondering, my Nirvana Foundation staff, with amazing pre-computer tenacity, unearthed an account in *The History of Santa Clara County* of a circuit preacher named John Johnston, who typically boarded with his parishioners while traveling from town to town. He never married and, in 1884, bled to death from an ax wound.

THE WHITE HORSE TAVERN

It was *The Montel Williams Show* that asked to film my visit to the reportedly haunted White Horse Tavern on the Hudson River in New York. Apparently workers were putting all the chairs on the tables when they left for the night and returning in the morning to find two of the chairs on the floor again, pulled up to a table where two shots of whiskey sat waiting.

All I knew ahead of time was that the White Horse Tavern was more than a hundred years old and that it had entertained an amazing clientele over the years, including Norman Mailer, Dylan Thomas, William Styron, Theodore Bikel, and Bob Dylan, some of whom were served their drinks for awhile by a bartender named Steve McQueen.

I understood from the moment I walked in the door what made such a noteworthy variety of people feel at home in this comfortable, unpretentious treasure of a place. Looking from the well-worn wooden floors to the embossed tin wall to the carved horse's head to the array of framed autographed photographs to the old wood and glass everywhere I turned, I found myself wanting to settle in and hang out for a few hours too, and I don't even drink.

The pub's owner had closed the doors to patrons for the hours we were filming there, so only Montel, his producers, and the camera crew were there. We were all in the same room, which made it easy for me to see that none of them could be the source of the rich, beautifully accented male voice I heard reading poetry from the moment I stepped in the door.

I asked the owner if someone else was there. He assured me no one was.

But I looked in the direction of the voice and finally noticed an unhealthy-looking, overweight man drinking at a table by a far wall. His eyes were deep set and drunkenly unfocused. He'd probably once enchanted everyone around him with his wit, his artistic command with words, and that gorgeous lilting accent. I got the feeling the enchantment had long since disappeared in the bottom of a shot glass and that he was indulging in a very deliberate process of self-destruction.

I described the man and my sense of him to the pub owner.

"That sounds like Dylan Thomas," he said. "He was only thirty-nine when he died of alcoholism, but God, did he look older."

I was so shocked that I thought he had to be mistaken—this bloated, dissipated man couldn't possibly be thirty-nine years old, let alone a world-celebrated poet who wrote, among many others, the exquisite "Do Not Go Gentle into That Good Night." But of course he would hardly be the first artist to commit slow suicide with drugs or alcohol, so I didn't argue. Instead I just watched that sad shell of a person until another impression hit me.

"He teased the waiter and waitresses a lot, didn't he? Especially by poking them?" I asked. The pub owner nodded, visibly impressed that I came up with that.

And then Dylan Thomas himself spoke up, slurred and proud to announce, "I once drank nineteen straight whiskeys in a row, you know."

It was tragic, not only that he'd systematically destroyed himself and was without a clue that he was dead, but also that, when he had so many genuine achievements to embrace, he was bragging about how he'd gone about it as if it were an achievement. He was earthbound, clinging to his self-destruction because it was familiar and not nearly as scary to his alcohol-clouded mind as the possibility of where he might be headed if he turned to the tunnel and let it take him away. I was studying him, looking for some hint of a thirty-nine-year-old man in that wreck of a body, when I saw movement out of the corner of my eye.

Both her hair and her dress were black, stark against pale skin unfortunately exaggerated by a heavy-handed layer of white powder. She had very small eyes, and her lips were shocking red, all an effort, I thought, to keep anyone from noticing that she wasn't beautiful but desperately wanted to be.

I psychically knew that her name was Marian Lee. She was in love with Dylan Thomas, and she spent her nights at the White Horse Tavern indulging his endless drunken monologues, hoping he would reward her devotion by noticing her and loving her too. He never did and never would, but as long as he's still there, she will be too, forfeiting the bliss of the Other Side to be where he is.

They both vanished before I could try to send them Home. Once they were gone I happened to take a closer look at the photographs on the wall. I now recognized that several of them were of Dylan Thomas, and I saw what had once been a sensitive, compelling face that could easily have inspired unrequited love. Directly opposite one of his photographs was a picture of an elderly woman—Marian Lee, later in her life, her eyes fixed on his from across the room. In the form of a framed, grainy photograph, he's looking back at her with the soft, welcoming smile she kept trying to inspire.

On the plane home from New York I read about the gifted, often tortured life of Dylan Thomas, which ended on November 9, 1953, five days after he allegedly claimed to have drunk eighteen whiskeys in a row.

I promise, it was nineteen.

He told me so himself.

MY OWN PERSONAL GHOST

I hope these stories haven't created the mistaken impression that my seeing and interacting with ghosts is an experience unique to me. Ghosts are everywhere, not as common as spirits, because more of us head Home when our bodies die than remain earthbound, but I can't think of a place I've been on earth when I haven't noticed at least a few of them.

It's almost embarrassing to admit this, but without a doubt my longest, most pervasive ghost relationship is with the one who's been living in my house since the day I moved in nine years ago. She's a young Native American woman named Falling Tears, and she died on this land in the early 1700s. Unlike most ghosts, she's happy as can be, stays mostly in back of the house, loves to play with the dogs, and is careful not to disturb anyone, although most of us have seen her: me, Angelia, Chris, Paul, Michael, and even a former assistant of mine who would much rather have shaved his head than experience anything supernatural that wasn't part of a movie.

What embarrasses me about Falling Tears is that in all these years I've never had any success with trying to "talk her over." She's so peaceful and content here, and so thoroughly convinced that she's still on her people's land, where she was born and where she spent a lifetime she loved, that she laughs off any suggestion that she doesn't belong here.

Francine is obviously well aware of this sweet, happy ghost, and she assures me she'll be retrieving Falling Tears and taking her Home "very soon." In Francine's world, where there is no such thing as time, it's impossible to guess when that might be. Until then, as ghosts and roommates go, we couldn't have asked for a nicer one.

THE DOPPELGÄNGER

This is for those of you who've been reading this chapter thinking, "Ghosts? Yeah, right," from a woman who used to say, loudly and with passion, "Doppelgängers? Yeah, right."

The word *doppelgänger* is German and translates to "double goer." According to legend, it's kind of like the ghost of a living person. Some people believe that everyone has one, and that only its originator can see a doppelgänger. Others believe it can be seen by everyone who knows the originator, which results in a lot of cases of mistaken identity and wildly creative alibis. Still others believe that the appearance of a doppelgänger is an omen of impending death. The common denominator, though, is that a doppelgänger is a person's living, breathing body seeming to bi-locate, or be in two places at once.

I'd read a little about doppelgängers as a literature major in college. Toward the end of his life the brilliant writer Guy de Maupassant allegedly took dictation from his doppelgänger for his novels and short stories, and one of my favorite classical poets, Percy Bysshe Shelley, was said to have met his doppelgänger one day while walking along the shore of the Mediterranean Sea. Shelley's doppelgänger simply pointed toward the water and then disappeared, and less than a year later Shelley drowned in that same sea.

Again, with no disrespect intended to Messrs. de Maupassant and Shelley—yeah, right. Spirits and ghosts made complete physiological and paranormal sense to me. If we believe that our spirits survive the death of our physical bodies, then the reality of disembodied spirits, whether they've transcended to the Other Side or not, is nothing but logic. But the living duplicate of a living human being? That made no sense at all. Besides, I'd been seeing spirits and ghosts all my life without a single glimpse of a doppelgänger, so clearly the whole myth was just plain silly, and I was happy to straighten that out for anyone who cared to listen.

God forbid I should keep my mouth shut when I'm wrong.

It was the middle of the night, and the heat in my bedroom woke me up. It was so hot that I was lying there drenched in sweat. Don't you hate that? And I also happen to be one of those people who can't get back to sleep for the life of me once I'm up, so I wanted nothing more than to convince myself that I wasn't really uncomfortable enough to get out of bed and end up awake for the rest of the night. It became quickly apparent that ignoring my discomfort wasn't an option—in fact, I was getting hotter, sweatier, and more miserable by the minute. Not one bit happy about it, I got up and went storming downstairs to the thermostat, ignoring as best I could the painfully hideous nightdress I was wearing, a gift from my mother with huge red roses all over it that looked like I'd been assaulted by a florist.

Some bonehead in the house had cranked up the thermostat to 80°, which I'm sure is heaven on earth if you happen to be an African violet. I cranked it down to something more in the human, energy-efficient range and turned to head back up the stairs.

And there, I swear to you, coming down the stairs, was me, from my damp, sweaty hair to my ridiculous floral nightdress.

I couldn't move. I couldn't even blink. Most of all, I couldn't make any sense of what I was looking at. I was so stunned that for several seconds I couldn't figure out which was the "real" me—the one descending the stairs or the one gaping at the one descending the stairs. And then—I can't come up with any other way to describe it—I slammed into myself at the foot of the stairway.

The next morning, after a long sleepless night, I started reading everything I could get my hands on about doppelgängers. I also talked to several colleagues, one of whom had also seen his doppelgänger and was as shaken by it and as mystified as I was. We were a little relieved to learn from our research that this phenomenon is relatively rare, but it's certainly not unheard of, and many

Me at six months of age.

At one and a half.
I loved sitting on tables.

My sister, Sharon, was afraid
of horses, so I had to stand
with her.

My beautiful grandma Ada Coil.

An older photo of Grandma Coil.

My precious Dad and me at a
father/daughter dance.

This was my school picture at sixteen.
I just had my hair cut and I hated it.

I loved to sit in the sun. Didn't know
it wasn't good to do that then.

With Joe, to whom I was engaged at nineteen, and one of my first loves.

This was my engagement picture at twenty, to my first husband, Gary.

My wedding to my first husband, Gary, who was a police officer.

With my friend and sister.

At twenty-nine, when I was teaching and pregnant with Chris.

Me with Chris, my psychic son, and Paul, my older son.

A family photo in the seventies during one of our vacations—Paul, me, Dal, Chris, and my foster daughter, Mary.

Taken right before I went on stage with some psychologists. When I'm nervous, I laugh.

Teaching with my second husband, Dal, during the beginning years of the Nirvana Foundation.

Larry and me on a California beach. We were not married at this time.

With my Novus ministers, who were there for Larry's and my wedding.

Chris, me, Dad, and Mom.

My fiftieth birthday party with Mom and good friend Barbara Crowther.

Larry and I were married in this photo. I was grateful he helped me out of my bankruptcy.

At a dress-up dinner during one of our Egypt trips with Larry, me, Linda Potter, Michael McClellan, Tina Coleman, Linda Rossi, and Nancy Dufresne.

Chris and me in our office when he started doing readings.

My oldest son, Paul, and me after a Thanksgiving dinner at my house.

Dal and me, who still remain friends.

Chris, Mary, me, and Mary's husband, Sparky, catching up with each other backstage at one of my lectures.

Me hamming it up for the camera.

Me with one of
my dogs, a male
chow named
"Peaches." Can
you imagine the
snickers he got
from the other
dogs at the park?

During filming of my pay-per-view special. My makeup was done by Kevin Aucoin, a dear friend, and I miss him very much. I wish he could have always done my makeup.

Two of my best friends, Shirley MacLaine and producer Nicholas Eliopoulos.

Montel and me playing around after a Halloween Montel Show in 1995. He is such a dear friend and has a great sense of humor.

Kate Linder, me, Michael Logan, and good friend Jeanne Cooper after one of my appearances on "The Young and the Restless." I have a new respect for every one of these daytime actors for how hard they work each and every day.

Montel and me after he produced my first pay-per-view TV special. I was so relieved when we had finished.

A recent photo of Larry King, whom I love, and me.

Sharon Stone and me after a meeting. What a spiritual light she is.

Suze Orman and me at Louise Hay's eightieth birthday party.

Zsa Zsa and me at a fund-raiser in Los Angeles for the homeless. She is very outspoken, but that's one of the things I truly love about her.

My sweet grandchildren, Willy and "Eya."
Getting them to sit still and smile at the same
time for this photo was a real challenge.

My darling
grandson, Jeff.

My granddaughter,
Angelia, and me
all dressed up for
Halloween. At
this age, Eya loved
to dress up in
costumes for any
occasion.

Angelia and me after running around exploring the mysteries of nature at a picnic in the park.

My precious miniature Dachshund, "Flower," and me. For the first six weeks after I got her, I had to sleep with my hand on her paw or she would wake up crying.

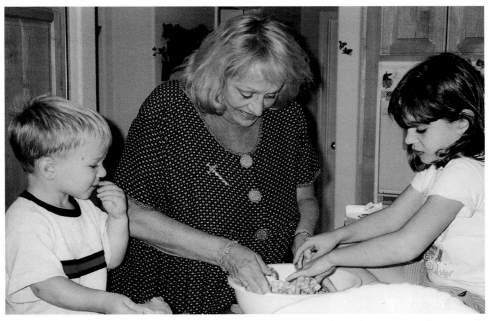

Willie, me, and Eya doing what came to be an annual tradition—making and stuffing the Thanksgiving turkey together. Willie got to stuff the neck cavity by himself because his hand was the smallest. Certainly not true anymore.

My final wedding, February 14, 2009, to the love of my life,
Michael Ulery, surrounded by my Novus Spiritus ministers.

My husband, Michael, and me on a cruise.

of those who've experienced doppelgängers are "normal" people. (I honestly have no idea what that word means, but in this case it refers to people who aren't accustomed to or even interested in the paranormal.)

At any rate, the fact is, I was wrong. Doppelgängers aren't mythical nonsense. I met mine, just once, without wanting to or intending to, and it's never happened again. Mind you, I still can't make physiological or paranormal sense of them. The only theory my colleagues and I could come up with is this:

When our spirits aren't inhabiting bodies and they're in their most natural form on the Other Side, one of their countless skills is bi-locating, the ability to be in two places at once. And our spirits don't lose their skills when they're incarnated; they're just temporarily restricted by the bodies they inhabit. Maybe—and I do mean *maybe*—on rare occasions our spirits feel like "stretching," and flexing the muscles of some skills they haven't been able to use for awhile, so they bi-locate for the sheer exercise of it. I can't imagine that there's any particular significance to their occasional appearance, since mine had nothing better to do than concern itself with a thermostat. The bottom line is, all I can say with absolute certainty is that, for whatever reason, doppelgängers exist.

Another bottom line: I've never met a ghost, no matter how happy or sad or angry or ornery or playful, who wasn't ultimately tragic in its lost, confused refusal to move on. When and if you find yourself living with one, or passing one on the street, it's understandable to be startled and maybe even frightened. But as you process the experience, please understand the ghost means you no harm, send it Home if you can, and, above all, thank it for the added proof it offers that, even when it remains earthbound, the spirit still survives death.

A BAND OF ANGELS

I was spending the night at Chris's house, helping him through a bad case of the flu. At around 3:30 in the morning I got up to get a drink of water. I walked up the hallway past the bedrooms and froze in place at the top of the long stairway. There in the massive foyer, filling every inch from the floor to the thirty-foot ceiling, was a glorious, impossibly beautiful Angel. It was radiant, with perfect skin that sparkled as if its body was lit from the inside. Its giant wings were at full span, brilliant white and tipped with silver. I was too much in awe to move or speak, almost feeling unworthy to even be looking at it. Then it slowly vanished, although its sacred presence was still palpable in the darkness.

That moment, which only lasted for a few slow-motion seconds, is and always will be one of the most humbling, cherished blessings of my lifetime. With all my heart I wish you'd been there with me.

LIKE YOU, I'M sure, I've loved Angels all my life. Long before I knew much about them, I knew they were the truth, I knew they adored us, and I knew they were God's special messengers whenever we needed them. Grandma Ada told me beautiful stories about them, the nuns taught what the Bible had to say about them, and I read every word I could find about them on my own. Then Francine came along, with more to tell about Angels than I dreamed there was to know, so that by the time the Nirvana Foundation became a reality I couldn't wait to spread the word to classes and study groups who were already as deeply in love with Angels as I was. In fact, polls were indicating that in the United States, a country of people who seem to have trouble agreeing on much of anything, more than 75 percent of us, regardless of race, creed, or political preference, believe in Angels. If that doesn't qualify Angels for miracle status all by itself, I have no idea what does.

────────

ANGELS ARE THEIR own species, God's divine legion of messengers and protectors. They never incarnate, and except for brief appearances on earth to intervene on our behalf, they spend eternity exclusively on the Other Side. None of us will ever become Angels, not because we're undeserving or because God loves and values us any less than He loves and values them, but simply because none of the spirits in His creation evolve from one species to another.

I know. I was a little disappointed at first too when I found out from Francine that no matter how tirelessly I devote myself to serving God throughout this lifetime, I'll never become an Angel. But the more I thought about it, the more I realized that my Angel aspirations had a whole lot to do with aesthetics—I mean, who among us doesn't want to look like what we all know Angels look like? In case your own memories of Home are a little hazy, though, let me help refresh them for you: Angels are androgynous, neither male nor female. Their bodies and their facial features are universally identical and incomparably, exquisitely beautiful. Their skin and hair color vary from one Angel to the next, so that the image of every race of humankind is equally reflected. Everyone who sees them, during their brief visits here or in their lives at Home, immediately notices exactly what I did that night in Chris's foyer: their skin seems to glitter from their pure, sacred essence.

Because the only emotion they ever experience is the sacred love of their Creator, Angels never change facial expression from one of utter placid devotion. They live among the general population of the Other Side, but unlike the rest of us, they don't socialize, work, or participate at all in the full, busy lives we enjoy there. Instead, they keep to themselves, never speaking, not even to each other, communicating only telepathically, with the sole exception of their magnificent concerts in the Hall of Voices, where all the Angels gather to sing hymns of praise to God's glory. Their hymns can be so transcendently soaring and joyful that they once pierced the veil between the Other Side and earth to announce and sanctify the birth of the baby Jesus:

> And there were in the same country shepherds abiding in the field, keeping watch over their flock by night. And, lo, the angel of the Lord came upon them, and the glory of the Lord shone round about them: and they were sore afraid. And the angel said unto them, "Fear not: for, behold, I bring you good tidings of great joy, which shall be to all people. For unto you is born this day in the city of David a Saviour, which is Christ the Lord. And this shall be a sign unto you; Ye shall find the babe wrapped in swaddling clothes, lying in a manger." And suddenly there was with the angel a multitude of the heavenly host praising God, and singing, "Glory to God in the highest, and on earth peace, good will toward men." (Luke 2:8–14)

Within the species of Angels there are eight levels of advancement, each level earned through experience. The more vast the body of experience, the higher the level of advancement. And the higher the level of advancement, the more powerful the Angel. New levels are earned through good works—protecting us, saving our lives, facilitating God's miracles, and carrying messages to us of the hope, joy, comfort, and love that are all part of our divine birthright. Angels are our direct link to our Creator, God's physical shoulders to carry us through fear, sorrow, and devastation until we can stand strongly beside Him again.

The eight levels of Angels can be physically distinguished from each other by the color of their wings. Each new color is earned and proudly worn as a reward for the Angel's increased body of experience. In ascending order, not of importance but of advancement and power, here are the eight levels:

1. *Angels* have wings that are a dusty, grayish white.

2. The wings of *Archangels* are pure white.

3. *Cherubim* wings are white with gold tips.

4. *Seraphim* wings are white with silver tips.

5. The *Virtues'* wings are pale blue.

6. The *Dominions'* wings are green.

7. The *Thrones* have deep purple wings.

8. The wings of the most powerful Angels of all, the *Principalities*, are brilliant solid gold.

The first seven levels of Angels are available to us at an instant's notice in a physical or emotional crisis. They can take the initiative themselves or be sent by God to intervene on our behalf.

The Principalities come only at God's command or if we specifically summon them. It's through the power of the Principalities that God performs His miracles and intervenes in our charts on the very rare occasions when He deems it to be in our ultimate best interest.

While all the Angels in God's divine army are watching over us throughout our lifetimes, we also select Angels of our own, just as we select Spirit Guides, to be our companions and protectors during our time away from Home. Depending on the difficulty of the chart we've written for ourselves, we might arrive on earth with, let's say, an Angel, two Archangels, and two Dominions. Unlike our Spirit Guides, our Angels aren't with us to act as our advisors and teachers. They've never incarnated, don't forget, so our human joys, sorrows, concerns, fears, and missteps are completely alien to them. But like our Spirit Guides, they don't accompany us here to change the course of what we charted for ourselves to learn and accomplish while we're here. They're not with us to see to it that nothing bad ever happens to us, that we and our lives are flawless from the beginning to the end of each lifetime we spend on earth. If our spirits could grow from perfection, we'd never leave Home in the first place. So even when times are at their worst, don't ever believe that your Angels have abandoned you. They're no more capable of that than God is.

I did "Angel shows" with both Montel Williams and Larry King, and the number of people who wrote and called wanting to share their stories of Angels who'd changed or saved their lives was overwhelming. No matter what the situation, the basic experience was always the same: during a crisis, a stranger arrived, seemingly out of nowhere, had a profound impact on the crisis—carrying a drowning woman out of the sea and delivering her safely to the beach, removing a trapped driver from a badly damaged car moments before it caught fire, laying hands on the forehead of a feverish child in the hospital seconds before the fever "coincidentally" broke—and then disappeared again before anyone could find out who they were or thank them. Thinking back on each experience, everyone involved realized that the stranger never spoke and had almost superhuman strength. And while in most cases the strangers looked fairly ordinary, there was something almost translucent about their skin and an inexplicable aura of loving peace about them.

It's absolutely true that when Angels descend for the specific purpose of rescuing us from an emergency, they assume a form that will call as little attention to themselves as possible. Sometimes they just appear to be a brilliant flash of light and other times remain completely invisible. I promise you, if all Angels arrived in the same breathtaking magnificence as the one I saw in my son's foyer that night, everyone around would be too awestruck to focus on the crisis at hand. So while they can't disguise the divine Light inside them that seems to illuminate their skin, or the aura of the purest, most sacred love that exudes from them, Angels will make every effort to fit into their surroundings, manifest themselves as a quick glow, or not physically appear at all when they come to save a life. And just to repeat in case this is confusing: Angels can and do temporarily take human form when they need to intervene on our behalf. But they never actually incarnate as human beings to live lifetimes here. (Yet another reason to envy them, but again, we're the species God created us to be, and it's our job to make the most of it with as little whining as possible.)

I've chosen a couple of Angel stories from the multitude that have been shared with me. It's no surprise that the ones that touch me most involve children:

My husband and I were on a family vacation at the shore with our eight-year-old son Jordan. Jordan is a good swimmer, so we felt safe letting him play and swim in the ocean close to the crowded beach. Suddenly an undertow grabbed him and pulled him down and out into the water, and he disappeared. I remember a lot of panic and yelling and people trying to get to him, and then I remember the sight of what I assumed was a lifeguard walking out of the ocean with Jordan in his arms.

He carried my son to the beach and laid him down on the sand while a crowd gathered around. Jordan coughed up a lot of water . . . and sat up within a few minutes. . . . I turned around to thank the lifeguard who saved his life, but he was gone. He wasn't among the crowd of people, he wasn't on the beach in any direction, he wasn't in the water again, he just wasn't anywhere. Everyone else started looking for him too, but we never saw him again. No one . . . knew who he was. He was tall and muscular, and his skin was very tan and kind of glistened, which I assumed at the time was because he was wet. But then I realized that all of us were wet and no one else's skin sparkled like that. Also looking back I realized that throughout the whole thing, he never said a word. I'm not asking if this was an Angel. I know it was, and I thank God every day for sending him to save my son.

Then there's this one from a grateful father about his son Jay, who'd been seeing his Angel all his life. In fact, Jay's Angel had become such a constant presence in his life that Jay named him Ball, after his favorite toy.

When Jay was six the family took a road trip across the country. Jay's father was driving, his mother was in the passenger seat, and Jay was in the back seat behind his father.

A car appeared from a side road, coming right at us, moving so fast there was nothing I could do. I knew that car was going to hit my door, and worse, my son's door, head-on, and all I could do was yell, "Jay! Get down!" Crazy as it sounds, I saw with my own eyes the other car suddenly seem to go into slow motion, and it ended up hitting the front left wheel well of our car as if it glided gently into us. Other than a minor jolt, we barely felt a thing inside the car. I immediately turned around to check on

Jay and saw him staring out the window with a look of awe on his face. He later told us that he saw Ball fly from the back seat beside him to the front of our car, push our car back, and then stand there so the other car would hit him (Ball) instead of us. Jay was afraid at first that Ball might be hurt, but, as he put it, "It turns out that Angels can't get hurt that bad," and in fact Jay was happy to report that Ball was just fine.

And no one in our family will ever forget the day that an Angel (I'll always believe it was one of the Principalities) saved my granddaughter's life. Chris, his wife Gina, and their daughter Angelia (nicknamed Eya, pronounced "EE-uh"), who was two years old at the time, had come with me to New York for a taping of *The Montel Williams Show*. Chris and I headed to the studio, where Gina would meet us after she and Angelia went shopping.

When she arrived with Angelia, Gina was pale, trembling, and sobbing so hard she could barely talk, while Angelia happily raised her arms for her daddy to pick her up. It took Gina several minutes to collect herself enough to tell us what had happened.

"We were crossing the street a block from here," she said. "We had a green light and the 'walk' sign, but you know me, I wasn't moving until I checked the traffic myself. I looked, it was all clear, and I took maybe three steps off the curb, pushing Angelia in her stroller, before, I don't know how else to describe it, it was like a pair of invisible hands shoved me as hard as they could back onto the curb. I was holding onto Eya's stroller, obviously, so she kind of fell backward with me, just as a car came screaming past us, right through the light, right where Angelia and I were before I was pushed out of the way."

She turned to me and added, "Mom, there was no one around to push me like that. And if I hadn't been pushed, there's no doubt about it, that car would have killed Angelia. I know it was an Angel. There's no other explanation. An Angel saved our baby girl."

I know it was an Angel too, just as every single person who's written or called or told me in person about an encounter with these divine beings has known, without wondering for an instant, that an Angel touched his or her life. Whether or not you've ever seen your Angels or sensed their presence, please love them and believe in them as much as they love and believe in you. And if you find yourself thinking that only "special" people are blessed with Angels, be assured that you're exactly right, as long as you also remember that in God's eyes, there's no one more special than you.

SPIRITS, READINGS, AND AUDIOTAPES

We learned very early on in the Nirvana Foundation that our most valuable tool, hands down, was the tape recorder. Some of you may still remember the kind we used most often: the old, reliable reel-to-reel recorders that weighed about six hundred pounds and couldn't have been less convenient to lug around. But for clarity and some truly remarkable experiences, it was unbeatable. I had to be dragged kicking and screaming into the world of the audiocassette recorder that, because of their portability, we were finally forced to start using.

According to a whole lot of research and, of course, Francine, it's much easier for the spirit world to travel from their dimension to ours when they have a helpful "conductor" to attach themselves to and kind of "ride in on," to put it badly. Electricity works beautifully, as does water, for example, which is why there's an increase in spirit activity during lightning storms. (You may have thought that was just a scary movie cliché, but it's an *accurate* scary movie cliché.) There's also an increase in spirit activity in the early morning hours of about 3:00 a.m. to 6:00 a.m., when the dew is at its heaviest and most useful. And, as I learned, sometimes by complete surprise, the magnetic quality of audiotape can bridge the two dimensions very effectively too.

————

I WAS DOING a regressive hypnosis session with a client I'll call Patricia. From the moment she went under, it was obvious that wherever she'd gone or whatever was happening, she was spellbound by it and not saying a word. And the longer she sat there in silence, the more I had a feeling I'm not sure how to describe—there was an intensity building in the room. I had no idea what was causing it.

Finally, to bring her out of the wordless awe she seemed lost in, I quietly said, "Patricia, look around and tell me where you are."

In a hushed, reverent whisper she began talking about a vast building with a massive dome and marble columns, and once she entered she found herself staring at countless wide aisles that went on as far as the eye could see, each aisle filled with more shelves than she could fathom, and each shelf filled with what looked like an infinite number of parchment scrolls.

I knew where she was, from Francine and from astral trips there myself. She was describing the Hall of Records, one of the buildings at the entrance to the Other Side. Patricia wasn't the first client to travel there during a hypnosis session. What was so remarkable was that, for the first and last time in one of those sessions, I suddenly realized that I was right there in the Hall of Records with her.

I kept quiet about it—any comment on my part would have amounted to leading her, which is strictly off limits. So I was listening to her tour and wondering how I'd been pulled along with her on this trip when she let out a little gasp and announced, "You're here with me."

I didn't confirm or deny it, and she went on walking us through that sacred, spectacular site. Before long I spotted a dark-haired woman with a classically beautiful face. She was draped in blue gossamer and was approaching us from two aisles away, not aware of our presence yet. She silently communicated that she was Patricia's Spirit Guide and that her name was Rachel. As she came closer, Patricia gasped again and announced, "Someone's with us."

It was hard to keep the excitement out of my voice—now there was no doubt about it, we really were on this trip together. "Who is it?" was all I said.

"It's a woman. She has dark hair and a blue filmy dress. I don't know why, but I think she's my Spirit Guide."

At that instant Rachel spotted us and called out, "Patricia!"

I bit my tongue.

"Did you hear that?" Patricia asked breathlessly.

"Hear what?"

"She said my name," she told me in a voice choked with emotion.

I was almost as overwhelmed as she was, but not nearly as overwhelmed as I was when I played back that part of the session audiotape later.

I clearly heard myself say, "Who is it?"

I heard Patricia's response, "It's a woman. She has dark hair and a blue filmy dress. I don't know why, but I think she's my Spirit Guide."

And then, clear as a bell on the audiotape, a third voice in the distance could be heard, saying, "Patricia!"

I'd never heard a spirit voice imprinted on an audiotape before. It was humbling and unforgettable. It also wouldn't be the last time it happened.

———————

MY RESEARCH TEAM and I were investigating a reported haunting at a wonderful old rambling mansion in New England. As always, we explored the whole house from top to bottom when we first arrived, and we found exactly zero signs of anything paranormal going on. I then settled into one of the upstairs bedrooms where the owners believed most of the ghost activity was centered, closed the door, turned on the tape recorder and sat there for several hours of absolutely nothing.

My team and I assembled again in the morning for a debriefing, and I rewound the tape and played it as we compared notes. It wasn't that big a surprise that no one else had experienced anything suspicious, let alone paranormal, all night either, and we declared it to be one of the most unhaunted houses we'd ever investigated.

What was a surprise was what we heard on the tape during that discussion, so loud and clear that we stopped talking and stared at the tape recorder. Somehow, while I was sitting there in mind-numbing silence hour after hour, the recorder was preserving the relentless, ear-shattering barking of what sounded like a very large, very nearby dog. I couldn't possibly have missed it. Neighbors for miles around couldn't possibly have missed it. And believe me, it went on and on and on and on and on, seemingly from the minute I sat down in that bedroom and hit the record button until the minute I left.

I asked the owners of the house about it. I asked the neighbors about it. I even asked the local police about it. No one had heard a loud, endlessly barking dog the night before, or ever in this area. The police had never received a single complaint about a barking dog, and in the end, no one in the area was aware of anyone who owned a dog larger than a miniature poodle.

After spending a long day searching for the invisible dog only a tape recorder could hear, I finally resorted to asking Francine what was going on. (I know there must be times when she sits there watching me, rolling her eyes over how hard I make things for myself sometimes when I could just check with her in the first place.)

"The dog on the tape was your white bull mastiff," she said, in a tone that implied a "you idiot" at the end of it.

Thinking I'd finally caught her in a glaring mistake, I smugly informed her that I didn't happen to *own* a white bull mastiff.

"Of course you don't," she replied, stifling a sigh. "Not in this life. But you did in a past life, and he's still with you from time to time protecting you."

I know that the vast majority of us have lived many past lives. I know that every animal we've ever loved from every life we've ever lived greets us when we arrive Home and never, ever forgets us or leaves us. But the spirit of a past-life dog staying around to loudly protect me would never have entered my mind. What more can I say but, "Duh!"? (And by the way, isn't that wonderful, comforting news? I've said this many times, and I don't mind repeating it: If our animals don't go to the Other Side, then I want to go where they go.)

———

WITHOUT A DOUBT the most spectacular display I've ever witnessed of spirit voices caught on tape happened on the night of a Good Friday remembrance at a lecture hall in San Jose. I was trancing Francine, who was telling the story of Christ's crucifixion at Golgotha. There were about fifty tape recorders in the room, and from what I was told later, Francine made the crucifixion so real, so wrenching, and so intensely present that everyone in the audience felt they were eyewitnesses in Jerusalem, grieving at the foot of the cross.

My phone was ringing off the hook before dawn the next morning. Six people, none of whom had talked to each other in the meantime, urgently needed to play me the tapes they'd recorded the night before, to see if I'd heard what they thought they were hearing or if they were just imagining things.

No, they weren't imagining things. What they were hearing, and what I heard, was unmistakable and impossible to miss. They assured me that the lecture hall had been completely silent throughout the

Good Friday service except for the sound of Francine's voice. I didn't need to be convinced—the slightest noise can break my trance, so the audience was told ahead of time that they had to be very quiet. But on six of the fifty tapes made that night, we could clearly hear a large number of people wailing and sobbing in heartbreaking sorrow as Francine's description of the crucifixion of Christ progressed.

Francine explained it as a phenomenon called a "bleed-through." A bleed-through, she said, is a profound, forceful convergence between the past and the present in which spirits experiencing a deeply emotional event come together in that dimension where time doesn't exist, where eternity is the only reality. In other words, the people in San Jose that night were among the throngs who mourned Christ at his crucifixion, just as those throngs were among the crowd in San Jose, bridging two thousand years with their united grief, clearly captured on six separate tapes in a room in which no one heard a thing.

––––––––

DR. BILL YABROFF, a psychology professor at the University of Santa Clara (now known as Santa Clara University), had become intrigued by Francine after attending several of her lectures. He asked if I'd be willing to let him test her. I had (and still have) enormous respect for Bill, and I trusted him to be fair and objective, so I welcomed the opportunity to let an "outsider" challenge her credibility for better or worse. He didn't tell me what the test was going to be, he just made a date with me in my office and at the appropriate time I relaxed into a trance and left him alone with Francine.

The test, it turned out, started with a list of twenty of Bill's now deceased patients, names randomly pulled from his files. As he read each name, he asked Francine to identify that patient's cause of death. His premise was that if Francine was genuinely speaking to him from the Other Side, she would have access to that information through the patients themselves. If she (I) was a fraud, she would be reduced to guessing her way through the list, which would guarantee that she'd fail the test miserably. As an added precaution, Bill avoided looking at the causes of death when he compiled the list of names and kept them on a separate piece of paper—that way, on the off chance Francine was reading his mind, he couldn't transmit information that wasn't in his head in the first place.

Bill and I listened to the tapes together later as he gave me the results. Out of twenty names, Francine had given an accurate, detailed cause of death for nineteen of them. And when I say detailed, I mean *detailed*. She didn't just say, "Gunshot wound to the head," for example. She said, "Self-inflicted gunshot wound to the right temple, with an exit wound behind the left ear." The one cause of death she "missed" was a drug overdose. Francine said there were three illegal drugs involved. The initial autopsy report only identified two. Just to be thorough, Bill called the patient's family, who informed him that a second autopsy had been performed and revealed a third drug that had contributed to the death of their loved one.

Bill was astonished by the test results. Frankly, so was I. I'd long since accepted Francine's legitimacy, as you know, but I honestly wasn't sure how she would perform "on demand." He started telling the story at his own lectures and conferences, always including the statement, "Sylvia makes the quantum leap." I take the same position now that I took then, even though I never did convince Bill to revise his conclusion: *Francine* makes the quantum leap. I'm just the messenger.

Bill never published the details of that test, but he did surprise me with a letter he took it upon himself to write "to whom it may concern." I've kept it and treasured it for all these years. It's on the letterhead of The University of Santa Clara, from William Yabroff, PhD, Director of Counseling Psychology, regarding "Qualifications of Sylvia Brown as a Psychic":

It is with pleasure that I recommend Sylvia Brown both as a person and a psychic. I have known Sylvia professionally for five years and find her to be an unusually authentic psychic as well as a highly ethical person, qualities which seem rare these days in the psychic field.

Sylvia seems to have the ability to accurately read the physical and emotional states of persons who come to her. She is specific in her readings rather than general, and encourages people to check out the specificity of these readings. I have referred a number of clients to her and have been gratified by the clients' reports of how helpful her sessions became in the course of therapy.

I have also had the opportunity to evidence her ability to find people and objects on a number of occasions. These include the finding of a valuable piece of jewelry, the location of metal objects underground, the accurate prediction of earth tremors and quakes, and descriptions of former structures which had been removed from the premise long before her services were called upon.

No psychic is 100% accurate and Sylvia is the first to call attention to this. Her own work reflects a surprising accuracy level and has inspired confidence with a number of professionals in Santa Clara Valley.

I recommend her for your most serious consideration, with enthusiasm and without reservation.

Thank you again, Bill, for everything. You have my eternal respect, gratitude, and friendship.

AS MY CLIENTS over all these years will tell you, I tape every reading. Each client gets his or her own copy, and many of the more unique tapes have become treasured archives of the Nirvana Foundation. I'm a firm believer that clients should be able to review their readings as often as they like, especially since I don't believe any reputable psychic should encourage or even allow clients to come back on a regular basis except under the most extreme circumstances. Psychics who exploit their clients by creating false dependencies, sometimes even addictions, by recommending readings once a day or once a week or even once a month are far more invested in their own well-being than that of the people who come to them for help, I promise you. I've always adhered to the idea that if I do my job properly, one reading every five years *at most* should give my clients all the guidance they need. When I hear someone say, "I found the greatest psychic—we spend at least half an hour on the phone every day," I want to grab them by the shoulders and scream, "Run!"

There's a common misconception that Francine and I essentially collaborate when I do readings. The truth is, except on very rare occasions when she might chirp a few brief, relevant facts in my ear, she doesn't participate. She views our lives in the context of the eternal journeys of our spirits, after all, so take it from me, her response to the day-to-day problems and crises we concern ourselves with on earth is likely to be (you can probably say it along with me by now), "Everything will work out as it's supposed to." I could devote every reading to saying nothing but that, and in the most cosmic overview of things I'd even be right. But my clients wouldn't find it any more satisfying than I do when Francine repeats it to me over and over and over again.

If you've ever wondered how you can develop your own psychic abilities, here's a three-step exercise you can practice by yourself or with friends whenever you like:

1. Ask a question, silently or out loud, to which you couldn't possibly know the answer.

2. Say to whatever you call your Higher Power, in whatever words you choose that remind you to get out of the way and receive the answer rather than coming up with it yourself, "Take it, God!"

3. Be willing to accept and repeat the first answer you get.

I know. It sounds simple. But trust me, steps 2 and 3 are harder than they sound. Keeping our own busy, opinionated little minds from leaping to answer questions, rather than stepping aside and quietly listening, isn't something any of us are accustomed to. And that challenge pales in comparison to the commitment to say out loud whatever answer comes through. Again I say, thank God for the audiotapes I've kept of some of my most memorable readings, because my staff has been endlessly entertained, not by my clients but by listening to me throwing myself open to making a complete fool of myself when it's time for step 3.

Many of you are familiar with one of my most glaring examples of an answer I no more wanted to say out loud than I wanted to shave my head, but it's worth repeating for those who haven't heard it before. The client was a lovely, well-dressed, perfectly groomed woman I would have guessed was a successful corporate executive of some kind. She had some concerns about her career, and before she could tell me what that career was, I received just about the last two words I would ever have expected: "worm farm." Can you begin to guess how much I didn't want to repeat that, and how strongly I was braced for this woman to march out of my office and demand her money back? But that's what I was given, so that's what I said: "You have a worm farm." And when she replied, "Yes, I do," as nonchalantly as if she assumed I see all sorts of people in the worm industry in the course of a day, I nearly fell off my chair.

It's been an ongoing source of curiosity among me and my staff that clients with similar, shall we say, "agendas" seemed to find their way to my office during the same time frame. For example, there was what we came to call Disrobing Week. One woman walked in and, without a word, immediately threw her blouse open. (Imagine my relief when it turned out she simply wanted to show me her new crucifix.) Two days later another woman came flying in, closed the door, lifted her dress, pulled her panties down to her knees, and urgently demanded, "Dr. Brown, take a look at this!" I never did find out what she wanted me to look at, and I didn't ask. Instead, I tepidly explained that I am not a doctor, I never have been a doctor and never will be a doctor. I'd be happy to refer her to a doctor if she needed one, but in the meantime, "Put your clothes on or get out of my office."

There was also what came to be known as You Name It, It's Possessed Week. Within a few short days I had a client who was convinced that her parrot was possessed by the spirit of her deceased husband, another client who was hoping I could perform an exorcism on his possessed vacuum cleaner, and still another client who wanted help with her possessed sponge. (Yes, a common household sponge. I was as stumped as you are about how you'd even know that a sponge was acting strangely, let alone that it was possessed.)

I'll tell you what I told them: first of all, I don't believe in possession to begin with. Yes, spirits can manipulate the behavior of animals, but they can't possess them, any more than they can possess any living being. And the closest thing to possession an inanimate object will exhibit is an imprint (which we discuss in chapter 8). For now let's just say that an imprint requires an emotionally potent history, and at least at first glance that would seem unlikely when it comes to vacuum cleaners and sponges. But probably the most interesting facet of You Name It, It's Possessed Week was the fact that not one of those clients was relieved by my assurance that no, they didn't have a thing to worry about, there was no possession going on in their homes. Every single one of them refused to believe me and actually seemed offended, as if they had their hearts set on owning something possessed and weren't about to let me spoil their fun. I'll be the first to admit it, too: there are some good laughs at me in those tapes of my trying to use calm logic on a woman who's yelling, "If you can't see that my parrot is really my late husband, then I guess you're not as psychic as I thought you were!"

Another staff favorite was the widower who just wanted reliable assurance that his dear, deceased wife was around him. I saw her right behind him, a radiant brunette with a prominent jaw line and small, deep-set hazel eyes rimmed by unusually thick eyelashes. He confirmed the description, but he still wasn't quite convinced, so he asked if I could tell him (translation: if she could tell him through me) the pet name they called each other.

I usually receive and repeat answers very quickly. When I hesitate, it's either because the answers come more slowly or because I'm not sure I'm hearing them correctly. This particular hesitation was because I couldn't imagine I was hearing correctly. But again, the commitment during readings is to transmit what I'm given, without editing or talking myself out of it when it sounds preposterous. So finally, doing the best I could with what his deceased wife was chirping at me, I said, "You called each other . . . it sounds like . . . 'smooshie'?"

It's hard to describe how silly it feels to look a total stranger in the eye, especially one with whom you're trying to establish credibility, and say the word "smooshie." It's even harder to describe how surprised and relieved I was when he lit up like a Christmas tree and yelled, "It's her!" It turned out their pet name for each other was actually "wooshie," but it was close enough for him—he took the position that if it had been sheer guesswork on my part, I would never have come up with anything that even rhymed with *wooshie*. And wow, was he right.

IT'S ALSO BEEN a source of confusion to me throughout the past half-century or so when clients react with such frustration when the deceased loved one they're hoping to contact doesn't show up but another deceased loved one does. I really do understand what it's like to yearn for some word—even a word like *wooshie*—from someone you desperately miss. But isn't any visitor from the Other Side better than none at all? I lost count not long after the Nirvana Foundation was created of the number of clients who played out some form of the following:

CLIENT: I'm hoping you can give me a message from my late mother.

ME: There's a woman standing right behind you. She's tall and very slender, with black hair, thick eyebrows and a prominent nose. She says her name is Alice.

CLIENT: That's not my mother, that's my aunt. I never cared much for her.

ME: Well, shall we hear what she has to say anyway, since she was nice enough to show up?

CLIENT: (sulking) As if we have a choice—we never could shut her up.

Now, first of all, how about some excitement about the fact that we're in the presence of proof that the spirit really does survive death, even if it's the spirit of that blabbermouth Aunt Alice? Let's face it, if that weren't true, how on earth would I know that the client even had an Aunt Alice who passed away, let alone be able to describe her? And second of all, maybe Aunt Alice has a message from the client's mother, or she can pass along firsthand how happy and healthy the client's mother is. Just as there are those of us here on earth who are more outgoing and communicative than others, the same is true in the spirit world. It's not uncommon at all that a "spokes-spirit" will act as a representative for other deceased loved ones during a reading, so honestly, chances are it will be worthwhile to pay attention to everything Aunt Alice has to say.

Nine times out of ten, by the way, the message from a deceased loved one is likely to be nothing more and nothing less than the news that they are alive and thriving on the Other Side—the greatest news any of us can ever get, after all. I can't tell you how rare it is that spirits arrive with messages like, "The will is in the bottom drawer of the rolltop desk," or, "My life insurance policy is behind the painting above the fireplace." And *never* do they show up and complain about what their casket was made of, or what you dressed them in for their funeral, or who ended up with their golf clubs. They don't care, and neither will any of us when we get Home.

―――――――――

I WOULDN'T EVEN hazard a guess about the number of clients who've asked me for messages from a deceased loved one, or reassurance that that loved one is happy and thriving on the Other Side, without realizing that more often than they might imagine, they're having very real reunions with those loved ones themselves and mistaking those reunions for dreams.

Grandma Ada had a great passion for dream interpretation, a passion she passed along to me. It was among the classes I offered for the Nirvana Foundation. I've written a book on this subject, so I'll keep it to a few basics here. And it's worth adding that, much like the fact that I'm not psychic about myself, I'm also not always adept at interpreting my own dreams. That's why I invariably tape-record an account of the dreams that really upset and/or confuse me so that I won't forget them, and then I share them with someone objective and skilled at simplifying the seemingly mystifying.

When I was at the height of my battle with Gary over the custody of Paul, Chris, and Mary, I had a dream one night that absolutely terrified me:

I was in a classroom. Paul, Chris, and Mary were huddled beside me, trembling. I was holding onto them in the middle of a protective circle I'd drawn on the floor. A parade of androgynous figures in faceless green masks was moving single file around the perimeter of the circle, chanting in a relentless monotone, "Beware of the three, beware of the three, beware of the three. . . ."

It was one of those dreams you wake up from in a cold, panicked sweat. It wasn't the green-masked figures that frightened me. They didn't seem menacing and never even glanced in our direction. But the "Beware of the three" message sent a chill up my spine. I was up all night, pacing and frantic, trying to figure out what "three" the figures were referring to. The only three I could think of were my innocent children. Obviously they meant me no harm, so what could I have to beware of from them? After hours of dark hazy thought, I came up with the theory that I wasn't being warned of pain *from* my children, I was being warned of pain *about* them. Which could only mean one thing: I was going to lose custody of them. I couldn't imagine surviving that, but what other possible interpretation was there? It must have been a prophetic dream, telling me to brace myself for losing the three children I loved more than my own life.

I'd maintained a great friendship with one of my advanced hypnosis professors who was brilliant about the subconscious mind, including the signals it sends through dreams. I was on the doorstep of his office, distraught and sleep deprived, when he arrived the next morning. He immediately sat me down and asked what was wrong.

I filled him in on the brutal custody battle that was consuming my life. Then I told him every detail about the dream, including the interpretation I'd come up with. I admitted, though, that between the stress of court and my lack of sleep, I wasn't thinking clearly, and it was imperative to me to sit down and talk to a friend who was. As

I explained to him, "If that dream was trying to tell me something and I lose this custody case because I didn't understand the message, I'll never forgive myself. So let's hear it, John. What do you think 'Beware of the three' means?"

"Who are you up against in this custody fight?" he asked. "Who's trying to take your children away from you?"

"My husband, obviously. And believe it or not, my parents have threatened to testify on his behalf. It's a long story. . . ." I trailed off, surprised to see a little smile on his face.

"Your husband, your mother, and your father, huh? In other words . . ."

I finally caught on. "In other words, three people teamed up against me. Three people I need to beware of."

I was instantly hit with a wave of relief. I knew that was the right answer. The dream wasn't a precognitive warning that I was doomed to lose the custody case. It was just a reminder to stay clear and focused on the three people who'd figured out that the surest way to hurt me was to separate me from my children. The fear that had been gripping me evolved into powerful clarity thanks to understanding that dream. My lawyer and I sharpened our focus on "the three," and it was during that process that I confronted my father and, of course, discovered that "the three" was really just "the two"— Gary and Mother. I was long past being afraid of either of them, and with Daddy on my side instead of theirs, I never had another shred of doubt that I was going to win that custody battle.

———

THERE ARE FIVE categories of dreams:

1. *Release dreams*, like the one I just described, which are simply our way of blowing off steam and confronting our fears in a healthy way while we sleep

2. *Prophetic dreams*, which are exactly what they sound like (and don't assume it's impossible for you to have those just because you aren't prophetic when you're awake—I've never had a prophetic dream in my life, so one has nothing to do with the other)

3. *Wish dreams*, which are also exactly what they sound like

4. *Informational or problem-solving dreams*, which explain why "Sleep on it" is usually very good advice when something's weighing on you, and

5. *Astral trips*, which really aren't dreams at all

It's as natural for our spirits to take temporary trips away from ours bodies as it is for our bodies to breathe, and three or four times a week that's exactly what they do while we sleep—what better opportunity than when our bodies are completely at rest and our busy, cluttered conscious minds are out of the way? Our spirits can travel anywhere they want once they're free of our bodies. We can drop in on loved ones on the other side of the world or on the Other Side itself. We can check on our childhood home to make sure it's being properly cared for. We can visit an ailing friend in a hospital across the country. We can revisit a past life or simply spend time at some favorite place at Home we've been yearning for since the moment we left to come here.

For example, I seem to be the most Homesick for the stunning domed, marble-columned Hall of Records at the entrance to the Other Side, since, as I mentioned earlier in this chapter, I've astrally traveled there many times in my sleep. I even had the experience once of wandering its infinite aisles of parchment scrolls until I found the chart I wrote for this lifetime. There was nothing dreamed or imaginary in the way my hands trembled as I pulled my chart from its shelf and unrolled it, only to find myself looking at a completely blank sheet of parchment. I was devastated and desperately confused until Francine explained to me that no one here on earth is allowed to read their own chart until after this lifetime has ended. I understand that. It would be like sneaking a look at the answers before taking our final exams, the ultimate cheating that would defeat the whole purpose of being here. I know. It's still frustrating. But it makes sense, and it also explains why you'll never meet a psychic, no matter how gifted, who's psychic about themselves. I can read your chart, but mine is off limits to me until I'm Home again.

Without a doubt one of the most informative astral trips I took while I slept happened just a few years ago, proving that none of us is ever too old or too well read to keep learning. It was so depressing that when I first woke from it I tried to convince myself that it was just a release dream, a series of images to symbolize some darkness I was wading through at the time. Unfortunately, it had all the earmarks of astral travel: it unfolded in chronological order, it was in color, and I caught occasional glimpses of myself taking part in it, much like "awake" astral trips in which the spirit and the body are two separate entities and the spirit can observe the body from a distance.

On this particular trip I had no idea where I was, but I knew it was desolate, oppressively gray, and eerily silent, despite the fact that I was surrounded by an endless crowd of spirits. They'd clearly left their bodies, but they weren't earthbound, and they were definitely too joyless to be on the Other Side. They ranged in age from adolescent to elderly, and each one of them seemed to be lost in a hell of deep depression, heads down, eyes lifeless and unfocused, shuffling in no direction without a word to me or each other.

Beyond these tragic souls in this awful place I could see a vast, looming opening that looked as if it would gleefully swallow anyone who came too close to it. It terrified me on sight, and I realized that it was the Left Door, the trap through which dark entities travel to recycle back into a fetus on earth without even a moment of the bliss, forgiveness, and divine Love on the Other Side. And somehow, instinctively, I knew that these heartbreaking spirits around me were in danger of plunging into that abyss if they didn't reunite with the faith they'd lost somewhere along the way.

In a panic, I began running from one soul to another on sheer impulse, hugging them and begging, "Say you love God. Please, just say you love God and you'll be free from this place. Listen to me, please, you don't have to be here, all you have to do is say you love God and He'll bring you Home."

Not one of those spirits even acknowledged my presence, and I still remember how hollow my voice sounded in the midst of that dead gray silence.

Then my own spirit fell back into my body and I sat bolt upright in bed. I was so relieved to be awake again, but it took me days to shake off the oppression of wherever it was I'd been. When I was finally ready to talk about it, I of course turned to Francine.

She told me I'd been to the Holding Place.

I'd never heard of it and demanded, "Why haven't you ever mentioned something called 'the Holding Place' before?"

"You never asked," she said.

Sigh.

The Holding Place, she explained, is the real purgatory I'd been taught about in parochial school. It's an interim destination between the Other Side and the Left Door, populated primarily by those who commit suicide. And let me rush on to stress that, contrary what many of us have been taught, suicide victims are *not* necessarily doomed to eternal damnation. Suicides motivated by revenge are guaranteed either a trip through the Left Door or a span of time as an earthbound to be trapped in the anguished pain they've left behind. Suicides triggered by mental illness, paralyzing despair, or genetic chemical imbalances beyond one's control have other options. Some make it safely Home. Others find themselves in that emptiness of the Holding Place, confused and heartbroken about their faith in and relationship with God. Their lifetimes on earth inevitably reflected that confusion, spent in that gray expanse between the dark side and God's divine Light and unable to find comfort in either. Through no fault of their own, they die neither turned toward God nor turned completely away from Him and arrive at the Holding Place uncertain which direction they prefer—recycling through the Left Door for another immediate incarnation or proceeding into God's waiting arms on the Other Side. And they stay in the Holding Place, stranded in hopelessness too deep for them to overcome on their own, until our prayers and the watchful spirits at Home give them the strength and the faith to find their way to the Light.

Since that astral trip that took me to the Holding Place, I've prayed every single day for those poor lost, desolate souls, and I ask you to do the same.

———————

THROUGHOUT HIS CHILDHOOD, my son Chris's favorite astral travel destination while he slept was another magnificent building at the entrance to the Other Side called the Hall of Wisdom. It is as sacred as it is beautiful, its entrance accessed by a vast mountain of white marble steps. Apparently it was the favorite destination of a whole lot of other children as well, unbeknownst to me until Francine suggested I have a chat with Chris, who was five at the time, about how disruptive giggling and rowdiness can be to an atmosphere of sanctity—it seems that his boisterous games of tag and peek-a-boo with friends on the steps of the Hall of Wisdom were disturbing the "locals."

A few decades later my granddaughter Angelia came along, and she chose the Hall of Justice and its legendary, unspeakably breathtaking Gardens for her astral trips while she slept. Beside the giant doors sits a statue of Azna, the Mother God. When Angelia was six years old she commented over breakfast that "in real life Azna has her hair in curls on top of her head, but in the statue she has it long."

Of course, astral travel isn't limited to our sleeping hours. I told you in an earlier chapter that Chris loved taking astral trips, asleep or awake, especially when he was bored, and he seemed to have passed that hobby along to Angelia. One night when Angelia was three, Chris, Gina, and I tucked her into bed, giving no thought at all to the balloon that was floating around her bedroom from a birthday party she'd been to earlier that day. We turned off the light, tiptoed out of the room, and headed quietly back downstairs to the den. We found it only mildly interesting at first, probably just an odd down-draft or something, when Angelia's balloon accompanied us from the bedroom to the den as closely as if one of us had it tied to our wrist. It hovered above us as we settled on the couch and turned on the television, and there were a few silly moments of asking the balloon if there was anything in particular it wanted to watch.

We paid a little more attention when Chris walked into the kitchen a few minutes later to get himself a snack and something to drink. The balloon didn't just go with him, it followed him from the refrigerator to the sink to the cupboards and paused wherever Chris did as if it were looking over his shoulder every step of the way. The longer this went on the more mesmerized we became, until Chris, out of sheer curiosity, started marching around the house with Gina and me following along as his incredulous witnesses. He leapt in and out of rooms spontaneously. He ran halfway up the stairs, then did a U-turn and ran back down them again. He made unexpected sharp right turns, stops and sideways moves. And at no time did his new pet balloon, never more than a foot away from him, miss a beat as it mirrored every step he took.

Chris had almost worn himself out when a possible explanation occurred to me—and it's worth repeating: I *always* want an explanation, even when there's nothing more than a headstrong balloon involved. I told Chris and Gina to follow me and led them back to Angelia's room, balloon in tow, and sat down beside her on the bed.

"Angelia, what are you doing?" I whispered.

She giggled as she answered, "Following Daddy."

———————

ONE OF MANY things I'm sure of in this life beyond all doubt is that Chris and Angelia didn't inherit their love of astral travel during waking hours from me. I don't like the feeling of being outside of my body. Like all of you, I take frequent astral trips when I'm sleeping, and I'm fine with that because my conscious mind is disengaged. And intellectually, I know it's a perfectly safe exercise; our spirits can return to our bodies whenever they want with no danger at all of getting stranded in midair somewhere. But usually, the instant my conscious mind catches on that my spirit is off on an adventure somewhere, it gives a knee-jerk "Uh oh" at the feeling that it's not in control and jerks my spirit right back into my body where it purportedly belongs.

Astral trips while we're awake aren't at all uncommon when we meditate, when we're under hypnosis, or even when we're in the midst of a deep daydream. I'm dedicated to daily meditation, and I'm disciplined about it, but part of that discipline involves staying just conscious enough to avoid astral travel as best I can. It usually works. Usually.

I was lying on the floor of the den one night, meditating to a Tantric yoga tape. I didn't know how successfully unconscious I'd become until I realized that my spirit had grabbed this opportunity to leave my body and was enjoying an aerial tour of the room, looking down at Dal, who was reading in a chair by the fireplace, and at myself, seemingly asleep on the floor. Then something brightly glistening in the air near me caught my eye, and when I realized what it was I literally gasped.

I'd been aware since my childhood in Catholic school of a Bible verse, Ecclesiastes 12:6–7, that reads, "Before the silver cord is snapped . . . and the spirit returns to God who gave it." I'd asked Francine about it, and she assured me that there is a very real silver cord, attached to each of us below the breastbone, that acts almost as an umbilical cord, keeping our spirits nourished and connected to our Source while we're away from Home. I thought it was a beautiful concept, probably not one meant to be taken literally but still beautiful.

And then, there it was, trailing from my spirit's solar plexus into the thin air of the dimension of the Other Side, a glittering silver cord, as fine and delicate as gossamer, twinkling almost invisibly but undeniably in the light from the fire in the hearth. It took my breath away, this visible proof that yes, we really do bear a physical connection to our Creator while we're slogging away through our lifetimes on earth, that He really does provide us with perpetual Parental sustenance every moment we're here so that we're never separate from Him.

I desperately wanted to share this miraculous sight with Dal, who'd dozed off in his chair by now. Trying to get his attention, I kicked the andirons on the hearth as hard as I could. Unfortunately, a good swift kick from a spirit foot amounts to nothing more than passing that foot right through whatever it is you're trying to kick, and a split second after that idiotically unsuccessful effort I found myself back in my body again, lying on the floor, still in awe after the blessing of a glimpse of my own sacred silver cord.

Dal stirred in his chair as I sat up.

"I don't suppose you saw that," I said.

"Saw what?" he asked.

(Move along, ladies, he's taken.)

So far, at least, witnessing my silver cord was a once-in-a-lifetime event. I've never seen it again.

But I have tape after tape of clients who've seen their silver cords. Many of them told me about it out of fear, confusion, or curiosity— they'd never heard of the silver cord and couldn't imagine what that sparkling thread was, one end of which disappeared into nowhere, or why it seemed to be attached to their breastbone. On rare occasions when I look back on the unplanned astral trip that led me to that fleeting, divine experience and wonder if maybe I just imagined it, all I have to do is listen to a few of those tapes and let my clients confirm it for me again and again and again.

In the late 1970s Francine began telling me about someone named Raheim who wondered if I'd be willing to channel him from time to time. On her recommendation, and out of my own intense curiosity, I agreed to give it a try.

Raheim is a highly advanced, powerful spirit on the Other Side. In his last incarnation on earth, he was a Sikh and a great teacher. He's not a second Spirit Guide. He doesn't chirp away at me on a regular basis the way Francine does, nor would I ever presume to ask him for guidance of any kind. My relationship with him is limited to the honor of his occasionally channeling through me for lectures, which by definition means that I've only been exposed to him via audiotape. He's brilliant, serene, and intensely compassionate.

Incidentally, I still remember the night my friend and collaborator Lindsay Harrison met Raheim. She'd met Francine several times, but Raheim was new to her, and as I was describing him I said, "And he's very . . ." At that moment all the lights in the room went out for a couple of seconds and came back on again, at which point I finished my sentence, " . . . powerful with electricity." We both laughed, and Lindsay commented, "So I see." The lights flickered off and on again one more time, we both said, "Thank you, Raheim," and the lights never flickered again that evening.

One of the most moving tapes of Raheim I've ever heard occurred at a large gathering at which I was channeling him. As often happens when I channel Francine, I'll always wish I could have seen this. In the midst of a beautiful lecture on some of the most intricate details of the Other Side, Raheim stopped talking for several moments and then said, "Come here, my child."

I was told later that he'd gestured to a little girl who was sitting with her mother in the front row. He pulled her into his lap (my lap, obviously) and held her, and for quite some time on the tape you can hear him praying very quietly without being able to make out exactly what he was saying. Finally, with a simple, "Amen," he released her, she went back to her seat, and he continued with his lecture.

The letter I got from her mother a few weeks later still fascinates me. Part of it reads:

> I brought my five-year-old daughter Maggie to a trance session with Raheim in the hope of a miracle after Maggie was diagnosed with cancer. Raheim focused exclusively on Maggie for several minutes, holding her and praying. And we got our miracle—at Maggie's next doctor's appointment after that evening with Raheim, her doctors could find no signs of cancer in her at all.
>
> What was almost as awesome to me as that true miracle was the fact that Maggie told me and her doctors that she was healed by a "man," that she absolutely saw a "man" healing her, even though of course it was Sylvia's body that was holding her. I've never corrected her, and I never will. She knows what she saw, and it's not the first time that her "vision" has been a lot sharper and clearer than mine.

There's a simple explanation for that, by the way: children, because they're newly arrived from the Other Side and by definition

are still more attuned to the spirit world than they are to the dimension of earth, are more psychic than adults will ever be. Isn't it sad
that so many of them are dismissed and/or told that they're imagining things, so that by the time they grow up they've been convinced
that their gifts are at best inappropriate and at worst "the devil's
work"? (Incidentally, to those who've hurled that accusation at me
from time to time: I'm much too secure in my relationship with God
to even dignify it with a response. And then, of course, there's the
fact that I don't happen to believe in the devil in the first place.)

I also want to clear up a common misconception about healings
and miracles, to make sure the Raheim story isn't misleading in any
way. Neither I nor anyone else on earth has the power to provide
healings or miracles, and anyone who claims to have that power is a
fraud. Healings and miracles are in the Hands of God and your own
name for what I choose to call the Christ Consciousness.

On those occasions when a healing comes *through* any of us, and a
miracle happens, we have no right to take credit for it. It's a sacred,
humbling honor when we're allowed to be a "transmitter," but that's
all we are.

It's important to remember that this earth we so fiercely cling to
as part of our mistaken fear that death is an ending is not really our
Home at all. We're simply here, briefly and voluntarily, to continue
the education of our spirits along an eternal pursuit of wisdom. The
Other Side is Home, and the death of our bodies that returns us
there isn't God's way of punishing us; it's His way of rewarding us
for accomplishing our purpose here and welcoming us back to our
real lives where we belong. When you pray with all your heart and
soul that a loved one not die, and it seems your prayers fail, don't
believe for one second that God ignored you or denied you or that
you didn't pray hard enough or deeply enough. Our prayers for the
survival of a loved one are granted in the greatest, most universal
sense of all, through the eternity that is our birthright. Through

God's eyes and through His promise, as hard as it can be to recognize through our eyes, survival has nothing to do with clinging to bodies here on earth that for whatever reason can no longer serve us well. Through God's eyes, the death of the body isn't cruel, it's a Homecoming.

The essential elements of healings and miracles, all of which need to be in perfect synch, can be oversimplified into the following:

- *God*, the essential Element of everything that exists

- *Prayer*, which is any open communication between our souls and God

- *Belief*, a word that transcends all religious rhetoric and dogma to mean nothing less than an acknowledgment of the flame of the divine spirit within us and its genetic connection to our Creator

- *Affirmation*, which is our awareness, conscious or unconscious, that the miracle of healing, like all things, is possible through God, as long as that possibility will serve the greatest purpose, whether that purpose is knowable to us at the time or not. It really all will make perfect sense when we're on the Other Side again.

- The *chart*, co-created by God and the soul for whom the healing is being asked before this lifetime began

If and when those elements are perfectly aligned, miracles and healings can and do happen. When they're not, we can hardly blame God or ourselves—we here on earth can be pretty short-sighted when it comes to what the words *miracles* and *healings* really mean, after all. While we've all chosen to be here as part of the eternal journey of our souls, the most miraculous healing we have to look forward to is waiting for us when we resume our perfect, blissful lives back Home.

The bottom line of this chapter: If you're even a little curious about spirit visits around your house that you might not be consciously aware of, buy a couple of audiocassette recorders, one for your bedroom and one for your children's bedroom, and simply hit "record" every night when you and your children are ready to go to sleep. I'm not about to guarantee that you'll capture spirit voices on tape, but take it from me and a whole lot of witnesses and researchers with the Nirvana Foundation, all it will take is one to convince you beyond all doubt that God meant every word when He promised us eternity.

SEVEN

MY VERSION OF HEALTH CARE

I was being wheeled in for minor surgery in Mountain View, California, when I looked up at the anesthetist and said, "Your wife's going to crash your car into a phone booth. Your wife will be fine. Your car won't."

There's no telling what this man had heard over the years from anesthetized patients. He just gave me a patronizing little smile, said, "That's nice," and pushed my gurney through the swinging doors of the operating room.

He was sitting beside my bed looking pale and upset when I opened my eyes in the recovery room. (Note to anesthetists: It's not confidence inspiring for your patients to wake up after surgery to find you looking pale and upset.) I asked him what was wrong and braced myself for news of some horrible mishap during the operation, like maybe they'd accidentally removed my liver or something.

"I just got a call," he told me, his voice trembling. "My wife hit a phone booth and totaled my car."

I was too relieved to sympathize and blurted out, "Oh, for God's sake, of course she did. Why else would I tell you that?"

He found this incident so amazing that he apparently told every medical professional in Mountain View about it, word spread from there, and that was the official beginning of a wonderful reciprocal referral relationship between me and what's grown to nearly 150 doctors and psychologists throughout the country. As you know, my psychic sensitivity to health issues started when I was a child. I had nothing to do with it other than repeating information I was given. The same is true now, of course, and I've learned a lot over all these years. That still doesn't make me a qualified medical or psychiatric expert, nor should I ever be confused with one. I know I've said this in other parts of this book, but I'll unapologetically repeat it: *Never turn to me or any other psychic as a substitute for fully licensed health care specialists, and never take ours as the final word on any physical or mental problems.*

Nothing proves more clearly that I'm not the source of the messages that come through during readings than the fact that, when the subject at hand is health related, I frequently have no idea what I'm talking about and have to dive for a medical dictionary as soon as the words have come out of my mouth. "You have too much iron in your blood," I told a client one day out of nowhere. "Double check this with your doctor, but I'd like you to eliminate dairy products from your diet and start taking L-Phenylalanine." She left, I looked up L-Phenylalanine once I figured out how to spell it and was pleasantly surprised to discover there really was such a thing. Two months later she wrote to tell me her doctor had concurred after a battery of tests and her health and complexion had improved remarkably.

I had a similar but much more serious experience with my nephew, Sharon and Richard's son Crisjon. I can count on less than one hand the number of times I've been able to offer psychic help, medical or otherwise, to members of my family, but this one came through loud and clear. We were all deeply concerned when Crisjon was diagnosed with osteomyelitis, an acute bone infection, that was going to require three weeks of hospitalization for constant intravenous antibiotics, followed by three weeks of recovery time at home in bed.

I was reassuring Sharon that Crisjon would get through this just beautifully when I glanced over at him across the room and suddenly knew there had been a mistake. "Sharon, get your son, we're leaving," I said with some urgency.

She stared at me. "What are you talking about?"

"Crisjon's doctor is wrong. He doesn't have osteomyelitis, he's in the very early stages of aseptic necrosis, which means an area of the bone isn't getting enough blood. It's much quicker and easier to treat. Forget this six weeks of treatment and recovery nonsense. Aseptic necrosis will run its course in about ten days with the right medication, exercises, and bed rest. Take Crisjon to my old friend Dr. Marvin Small and get a second opinion. I'm sure he'll agree with me, but even if he doesn't, it's worth a try, right?"

It wasn't easy, but Sharon and Richard managed to liberate their son from the hospital and take him to Dr. Small, where tests and X-rays confirmed that he was suffering from aseptic necrosis. After following Dr. Small's orders to the letter, Crisjon was back at school two weeks later.

And if you think that, left to my own devices, I would have known what osteomyelitis was, or aseptic necrosis, or how to tell them apart, let alone how to treat them, you're giving me credit I definitely don't deserve.

Typically, when I receive information and understand it clearly, it comes in very quickly, whether I'm expecting it or not. A perfect example was a client who came to my office for a reading having nothing to do with medical issues. She looked normal and healthy, so I was as shocked as she was when I suddenly yelled, "Don't sit down! We've got to get you to a urologist!"

She couldn't have been more frightened (and who could blame her?) as I rushed her to a doctor friend of mine. He called me a couple of hours later to say it was a good thing I'd brought her in—she had an advanced bladder infection and would have been in serious trouble without immediate treatment.

Which brings to mind a story of how great I am at ignoring my own advice.

I don't think there's any question that there's an intricate connection between our bodies and our minds, and I started paying close attention to how literally our health can be affected by our environment. That specific thought first entered my mind when I went to the hospital to visit my dear friend Dr. James Cochran, who was dying of bleeding ulcers. I asked him how this happened, and he said, so sadly, "I don't know Sylvia, I guess I just can't stomach life any more." He didn't notice the ulcer-stomach connection when he said it, but I started paying attention to clients whose bodies were yelling at them in some way about life issues they were struggling with. For example:

- Chronic neck problems? Who or what is the pain in your neck?

- Failing eyesight? What in your life are you trying to avoid looking at?

- Hearing starting to fail? What in your life are you trying not to hear?

- Dizzy spells? Who or what is keeping you off balance?

- Chronic breathing or bronchial problems? What do you need to get off your chest?

You get the idea. And I've found it helpful with any number of clients over all these years. In fact, it's not unusual for a lightbulb to go on over their heads the minute I hear the complaint and ask the relevant question. Much like when the same thing happened to me.

I was seeing my own doctor, Dr. Jim Fadiman, an old friend who knew my work and had also found that literal health/environment discussion very useful with his patients. I'd made an appointment about a recurring bladder infection I'd been struggling with for weeks. After he examined me and listened to my list of symptoms he said, "Okay, tell me, what's going on with you?"

Without giving it a single thought, I answered, "Oh, nothing much. My mother's just pissing me off again as usual."

And I wondered why I was having a bladder problem? Duh. It even took me a minute to figure out what Jim was laughing about.

I also believe that, because of the power of the signals sent from the subconscious to the body, we sabotage our health in all sorts of other subtle ways besides involving ourselves with negativity. If you listen closely to yourself and those around you, you might be surprised at how often phrases slip into conversations that could easily cue your very literal body into reactions you never intended:

- "He/she/it broke my heart."

- "He/she/it is killing me."

- "He/she/it is going to give me an ulcer."

- "He/she/it makes me sick."

- "He/she/it wears me out."

- "I'd rather die than . . ." or its close relative, "I'd rather lose an appendage than . . ."

- "I can just look at (name your favorite junk food) and gain weight."

There are countless examples of how carelessly and needlessly we run the risk of compromising our bodies with what boil down to health-related "facts" and/or "predictions" we really don't mean at all, essentially jinxing ourselves for no good reason. Even if you don't believe me that it makes a difference, just humor me and develop a superstition against it instead, and correct yourself and those around you every time that form of negative programming slips out of your mouth.

———

ANOTHER FASCINATING MIND-BODY connection that started filling the Nirvana Foundation files was an observation that became too consistently apparent to ignore. It's indisputable that trauma has a debilitating effect on our health. When we're not paying attention, we all make the mistake of using our bodies as emotional dumping grounds. But the more readings I did that had anything to do with illness, the more I realized that our bodies are very specific when it comes to how and where trauma is likely to affect them.

Health issues from the chest up, such as head colds, ear and sinus infections, upper respiratory inflammations, bronchitis, and heart problems, when they don't start from any obvious environmental source, are most often caused by a sudden trauma. If you're suffering from any illnesses in that area of your body for no apparent reason, look back to your recent history for the death of a loved one, a divorce or breakup, the loss of a job, an unexpected financial setback, destruction of property from a fire or natural disaster, a seemingly injury-free car accident or any other jarring event. Once you get to the source of the trauma and make the connection between that and your current "from the chest up" problem, you'll be able to treat the problem much more efficiently.

Illnesses originating between the waist and the chest, such as acid reflux, ulcers, chronic indigestion, and/or stomach cramps can be indications of more deep-seated traumas, issues we're trying to "push down" out of sight or out of our immediate consciousness rather than address and heal from: unresolved conflicts, overdue apologies, unacknowledged guilt or anger, chronic stress and/or unhappiness at home or at work, and self-inflicted anxiety from procrastination, for example.

Health problems from the waist down—colitis, problems with the reproductive organs, chronic constipation or diarrhea, intestinal cramps, hemorrhoids, and such—can most often be traced to a trauma in childhood or in a past life, something the conscious mind probably isn't aware of but the subconscious mind is holding onto and needs to release.

The subject of physical health gives me a perfect opportunity to address a frequent question about these charts I keep talking about: if we map out every minute detail of the lifetimes we're about to live before we come here, doesn't that eliminate the whole idea of free will? The answer is, No, it doesn't.

Just as we chart negativity into our lives to learn to face up to it and overcome it, we also chart illnesses as a series of tests to see how we deal with them and teach us to be our own most vigilant advocates. As a simple example, let's say we chart a cold for ourselves. We can attack it and take care of it, or we can do nothing, be careless and neglectful, and let it blossom into pneumonia. The choices are ours, working from the basics we designed before we came here, and the mistakes we make along the way are inevitable, challenging opportunities for growth.

My gift for doing psychic "health scans" has been second nature to me for as long as I can remember, and I cherish my collaborative relationships in the medical community and the mutual trust we've built together over all these decades. The same goes for my relationships in the psychiatric community, although the phrase "second nature" hasn't always applied to those clients.

Psychiatric referrals were an interesting challenge from the very beginning. The problems are often subtle, more deeply hidden, obviously, and typically require a much more cautious approach than physical problems. Regressive hypnosis, or hypnosis of any kind with someone with a mental illness, can only be practiced by a licensed psychiatrist, so that isn't an option. Besides, it's not always practical when something more immediate is called for.

My very first referral from a psychiatrist was a girl in her teens. Her doctor thought her problem might be more in "my territory." It seems she was being haunted by a shadowy figure that was attached to her and following her everywhere she went twenty-four hours a day, with the ultimate intention of hurting or maybe killing her. She was so terrified of it that it was destroying her life. She quit school and would only leave the house for therapy appointments. She couldn't eat or sleep, she was severely depressed, and she was desperately in need of help the psychiatrist had been unable to give her.

I anticipated meeting a girl who was experiencing a haunting by some poor confused ghost who'd become fixated on her for some reason, and I was ready, willing, and able to deal with it. It surprised me when she walked in with no ghost or any other entity around her at all, despite the fact that she resolutely believed it was there and pointed it out to me.

Now what? This was my first psychiatric referral. I wasn't about to let her or her doctor down, so without a ghost to take on, it was time to improvise. I prayed with her. I led her through a healing meditation. I even resorted to performing an exorcism despite the fact that I don't believe in them. And I got exactly nowhere.

Finally I did what I should have done in the first place: I sat back, closed my eyes, and silently prayed, "She's all Yours, God. I'm fresh out of ideas. Please help her and just tell me what to do to make that happen."

My prayer was answered instantly. Suddenly I knew exactly what this girl needed, and believe me, I would never have thought of it myself. I opened my eyes, studied her as if I were seeing her for the first time, and announced with a convincing gasp, if I do say so myself, "Oh, look! You were absolutely right, there *is* someone attached to you! I can't imagine why it took me so long to see him. And guess what. He's not here to harm you at all. In fact, he couldn't if he wanted to. He's just a little boy."

Her mouth dropped open. "A little boy?"

"He's adorable," I said. "He's only nine years old, and he's very frightened because he's lost. He's staying close to you hoping you'll take care of him."

She thought about that and finally smiled. The tension left her face, and her voice filled with compassion. "I can handle a little boy."

By all accounts, after she left my office she slowly started resuming her life again. It was indeed much easier to ask a little boy to please play by himself when she was busy, and to wait for her at home when she went out, until he simply went away one day and she never saw him again. The last time I heard from her was a thank-you note enclosed with the announcement of her graduation from college.

It was a great lesson about fear: when someone is afraid of something, rather than telling them they're being ridiculous or imagining it, find a way to reduce it to something they know they can handle. Or, if you must, do battle with it yourself on their behalf.

A few months later, a referral came in whom my staff and I still affectionately call "the snake woman." A clinical psychologist in the Midwest sent her to me after many unsuccessful therapy sessions in which he'd tried to convince her that, contrary to what she believed with all her heart, she really didn't have a snake wrapped around her waist. The fact that snakes were her greatest terror on earth made this a pretty dramatic nightmare for her, and the psychologist had had no luck convincing her that there was no snake and/or unearthing her basis for thinking she was sporting a live snake for a belt.

I had no idea how I was going to approach this poor woman, but I did pray for guidance, with a promise to God that I would do whatever it took to help her if He'd just let me know what that was. I took it as an answered prayer when, a moment or two later, she stepped into my office and out of nowhere I heard myself shriek, "Oh, my God, you've got a snake around your waist!"

My promise to do whatever it took wasn't made lightly—throwing dignity to the wind, I proceeded to grab that imaginary snake from around her waist, wrestle it all over the office for several minutes, and finally beat its imaginary head to death against the wall. It was worth my feeling ridiculous to watch her walk out a half-hour later happy and almost weak with relief.

I took my cue from that success to deal with the woman who was about ten steps past stressed out because her eyeglasses wouldn't stop talking to her. I didn't let her know that her psychiatrist, who sent her to me, had already explained the problem before she got there, and I managed not to look skeptical as she told me about these glasses she was stuck with that were driving her crazy because they just wouldn't shut up. I took them from her, held them to my ear for a minute or two, and then gave them back with a dismissive, "No wonder they're driving you crazy. Talking is one thing, but they're so boring!"

Curious, she put them back on, listened and said with surprise, "They are, aren't they?"

I don't know whether or not her glasses kept talking to her, but I do know that she immediately stopped listening to them now that she'd realized they had nothing of interest to say.

You'll never hear me claim that I'm able, or qualified, to diagnose and treat psychiatric referrals on a long-term basis, but it's enormously gratifying to help clients past some hurdle that's getting in the way of their progress. And this seems like an appropriate time to thank the psychologists and psychiatrists who've been a Godsend to the clients I've referred to them as well, and who've been invaluable, stimulating consultants, collaborators, and friends over all these years. Here's to our many more years ahead.

EIGHT

BROADENING HORIZONS

I t was the 1980s, and life was exciting. The Nirvana Foundation was busy and thriving. My marriage seemed solid, and my children were en route to becoming grownups whether I wanted them to or not.

Mary had been a wonderful daughter, sister, student, and friend and left us when she was nineteen to marry a lovely guy. Mind you, he wasn't good enough for her, but in our eyes, no one was good enough for her.

Paul had started his teenage years with a little kinetic energy problem that passed when he was (finally!) finished going through puberty. For those of you who don't already know this, kinetic energy is an unintentional, spontaneous influence over inanimate objects, with the result that the person who finds himself possessing it becomes an occasional, hapless force field. In Paul's case, every night after he went to bed I would hear a long, loud series of thudding noises coming from behind his closed bedroom door. I quickly discovered that, through no fault of his own, some combination of his kinetic energy and his falling asleep was causing every shoe he owned to career wildly around the room, bouncing off the walls and ceiling and keeping everyone in the house awake but him. All I had to do to quiet things down was knock loudly on his door and yell,

"Paul, wake up and stop that!" It only took a few months for either his hormones to calm down or for him to learn to control his kinetic energy, I was never sure which.

Paul was a smart, popular student, a track star with lots of friends. Chris was a great student as well, as popular as his brother and a standout in wrestling and soccer. They were distinctly different from each other: Chris was a fashionable dresser, for example, whose closet was always in impeccable order, while Paul preferred comfort over fashion and what I'll politely call a more laid-back approach to tidiness. We always had a house full of kids, and I enjoyed every minute of it. I was especially grateful that Daddy, whom they called Poppy, was around and able to be such a big part of their lives.

Like most of you who have more than one child, I'm sure, I noticed very early in their lives that there were and are subtle differences in my relationships with Paul and Chris that became more obvious as they got older. Neither of my sons is less important to me or less treasured with all my heart and soul. Some of the differences are attributable to the unique person each of them is. But in case you've ever wondered about this kind of thing between you and your children, here's a more significant part of that particular puzzle.

Paul, Chris, and I have all gone through hypnotic regression— separately, of course, so there was no danger of influencing each other's experiences.

Paul remembered one and only one past life. It was in Naples, Italy, in the 1500s, and he was probably physically challenged in that life, since the moment he "arrived" there, his head twisted to the side and drooped as if his neck was having trouble supporting it. I was his mother, and I devoted that lifetime to taking care of him.

Chris, on the other hand, has been scampering around on this earth time and time and time again, and he and I have been together in three other lives before this one. We were husband and wife in England, where he lodged me in a beautiful castle and saw to it that

I had everything I could possibly want . . . provided I didn't set foot outside our massive, luxurious home. Next we were brother and sister, living on a successful vineyard in what was then Czechoslovakia. And finally we were cousins in India, raised together so that we might as well have been brother and sister again.

So how big a surprise is it, really, that Chris and I have always seen to it that we live very close to each other and that he's intensely protective of me, while Paul and I adore each other but have never felt the need for quite as much geographical proximity or daily involvement in each other's lives?

None of which has anything to do with the subject at hand, but you see what happens when I start talking about my children? Back to where I was headed at the beginning of this chapter.

ONE DAY OUT of nowhere, a client and her husband, Robbie and Dr. Ian Stewart, who had moved to Kenya, invited Dal and me to come for a visit. We couldn't afford the time off or the expense, but we were on a plane to Africa before we had a chance to talk ourselves out of it.

I referred earlier to morphic resonance, that relative of cell memory in which you arrive in a place you've never been or read a thing about in this lifetime and instantly feel as if you've come home. My first undeniable experience with morphic resonance happened when we stepped off the plane in Kenya. I didn't just fall in love at first sight with everything about it, I felt as if I'd been missing it terribly all my life, and I knew my way around a few areas that were as familiar to me as my old neighborhood in Kansas City—not psychic knowledge, but my spirit remembering.

A Nairobi journalist, Kathy Eldon, arranged through our hosts to interview me. Bless her heart, she was as curious as every good reporter should be, but she didn't particularly believe in psychics and was politely tolerating me when we started. So I did something I often do when I want to put the issue of my credibility to rest so we can relax and enjoy ourselves—I talked about her. As she wrote later in the Kenyan newspaper *The Nation*:

Suddenly, in the middle of our conversation, [Sylvia] . . . told me how many children I have, their sexes, and gave accurate descriptions of their personalities. She discussed a trip I would be making, which I had planned only the day before. She talked about a book I would be writing and discussed medical complaints I had experienced in the past. She used words to describe me that only my best friend would have chosen, and pinpointed an incident two years back which led to my present job. I was astounded. Sylvia had no way of doing research on my life, and indeed, much of the information she imparted was known only to me.

I'd clearly won her over, since she went on to introduce me to two extraordinary men. One was an Oxford don named Mark Horton, who had excavated ancient ruins throughout Kenya and off the coast in the Indian Ocean. Again, I'm convinced that it was spirit memories rather than psychic information when I successfully identified the dates and origins of the coins he showed me, and I was fascinated by him and his work.

The other introduction Kathy Eldon treated me to was Dr. Richard Wilding, Director of Coastal Sites and Monuments at Kenya's National Museum. The three of us traveled to the ruins of Gedi, a city that was mysteriously evacuated in the seventeenth century and remains deserted today, overseen by the museum. No one knows what happened to the seemingly prosperous twenty-five hundred or so people who lived there or why they apparently abandoned this once beautiful place so quickly and completely. After we'd toured the empty, exquisite city for awhile, Dr. Wilding—another polite skeptic—asked if I had any feelings about why everyone left their homes and their lives in Gedi all those centuries ago. I told him what I still believe to this day: something polluted the water system, and many people died. The rest of them moved away out of fear and never came back.

His response was the most enthusiastic I'd heard him all day. "Yes! Yes! That could account for the exodus very well indeed!"

I doubt that I was the first to come up with that theory, but it was apparent that I'd made some headway with him by not suggesting a mass alien abduction or whatever other looniness he'd been braced for. We parted ways that day with a lovely mutual respect I'll always appreciate.

I owe a lot of my ongoing Kenyan and other international connections to Kathy Eldon. When I went to Kenya again the following year, it was thanks to her articles and contacts that I had the pleasure of doing a reading for Philip Leakey, a member of Parliament and the son of Louis and Mary Leakey, the world-renowned paleontologists. During the reading I had a horrible vision of potential harm coming to Kenya's president Daniel Moi. I saw President Moi in Mombasa, surrounded by flags. "He shouldn't be there," I told Mr. Leakey. "He's in a fairground, as we call it in America. Someone there wants to hurt him. He shouldn't go."

President Moi put in an official appearance at an annual festival in Mombasa a few months later, and thanks to Philip Leakey taking me seriously and warning the appropriate people, Moi surrounded himself with extra security and cut his visit short. Obviously we'll never know if I was right about the impending danger, but in cases like that I'm perfectly content just to wonder.

I'm proud to say that I was given the Kenyan Kikuyu title

"Mumbi–1," which translates "First Woman of the World." I've visited that magical country again many times and, as an added bonus, come home with more input for the Nirvana Foundation.

––––––––––

IT WAS A few years later, and this time Dal and I met Ian and Robbie Stewart at Tree Tops and Keekorok, a lodge off the Serengeti. In the middle of our first night there someone jarred me out of a sound sleep by bumping hard against my bed. I sat up to find a very handsome, extremely upset East Indian man in a white turban standing at the foot of the bed. He was so solidly materialized that it took me a minute to realize that no, he wasn't part of the lodge staff; he was a very distraught ghost. I reached for Dal and gently shook him, wanting to share this experience with him. He went right on sleeping, so I focused on the Indian man again.

"Mem-sahib, please, you must help me," he said, trembling and wringing his hands. "I am so afraid for my family. I know you can see me."

"Yes, I can see you, and of course I'll help you, if you'll tell me how," I assured him.

"They're coming for us. We will all be dead by morning."

I opted not to tell him that he and his family were already dead. I knew that his family was safe and happy on the Other Side, so I decided to see if I could urge him into a frantic enough search for them that he'd find his way Home out of sheer desperation.

"Then leave! Go! Get out of here and find them!" I yelled.

He instantly vanished. I looked at my husband, hoping he'd at least been awake long enough to see the man disappear. Instead, Dal began snoring. (Show of hands—how many see a long-term future for this marriage?)

The next morning we met Ian and Robbie in the dining room for breakfast, and I told them what had happened during the night, only shooting a quick glare at Dal when he said, "Why didn't you wake me up?" The fact that Dal had slept through the whole thing, including my yelling at the man to go find his family, seemed to make our hosts a little skeptical, until the maître d' stepped up to the table.

"Forgive me, mem-sahib," he apologized with a courteous bow, "but I couldn't help overhearing your story. Are you aware of what happened on this very spot almost twenty-five years ago?" I shook my head, and he continued, "A group of rebels from what was thought to be an offshoot of the Mau Mau descended on the town and brutally massacred the East Indian population. It was a great tragedy."

My breakfast companions were gaping at me. I pointedly ignored them as I gave the maître d' what might easily have been the most generous tip of his career.

I'm thrilled to add, by the way, that the beautiful Indian man did find his way Home to his family, not that night but a few years later. Whoever talked him over: God bless you.

It was also in Kenya that I learned about a very rare, exquisite group of spirits called Mystical Travelers. They're advanced souls who, when they're on the Other Side and ready to incarnate again to gather and teach more wisdom for God's service, don't limit themselves to another lifetime on earth but instead essentially say to their Creator, "Wherever in this universe you need me, I'll willingly go." They usually live several lifetimes here but are then ready to graduate to any other inhabited planet where God feels they're most needed, and their purpose is usually to touch and transform lives rather than to be touched and transformed themselves.

Francine explained Mystical Travelers to me after an extraordinary experience that was shared with me by my Kenyan friend Oona. Oona had a son named Jared who, from the moment he was born, seemed uncommonly serene, wise, and sensitive. Happy as he was, there was an obvious sacred Light in his huge brown eyes and a sense that he arrived here knowing more than most of us adults could ever hope to learn. I love being around most children, but I always felt uniquely honored to be in his presence without quite understanding why that was.

Jared was diagnosed with leukemia when he was four years old. Shortly after his fifth birthday, it became heartbreakingly apparent that he was ready to go Home. Oona slipped into bed beside him and held him as tightly as the tubes in Jared's tiny body would allow. In her few short years with him, his courage and his deep, unquestioning connection to God and the eternity of his spirit had given her a faith she'd never imagined before he came along. As she lay there in silence with him, her prayers weren't about the bitter unfairness of losing such a precious child so soon; they were prayers of gratitude for blessing her with every minute she'd been given with this very special soul.

She felt him lift his head to bring his mouth closer to her ear, and she could barely hear him as he whispered, "Mama, I'm going to God now. Please hold my hand."

She took his hand, and at that instant she felt his powerful spirit rise up from his body. There was fearless awe in her voice as she described the realization that he was pulling her spirit up from her body as well. He didn't take her to the tunnel that was waiting for him. Instead, holding firmly to her hand, he took his mother deep into the night sky. She was wide awake and never more joyfully alive as she soared with him through what seemed like millions of diamonds on an endless sea of black velvet, and when she looked into his eyes that were sparkling with life again, he smiled blissfully back at her and said, "I just wanted to show you the stars before I go Home."

A blinding golden-white Light gradually ignited among the stars, and from deep inside it a handful of beings started toward them. Oona couldn't see their features, but she knew with sacred, peaceful certainty that they were coming to welcome her beloved boy. She heard him say, "Thank you, Mama, for coming this far with me." And then he squeezed her hand, let go of her, joined the beings who were so happily gathered around him, floated away with them, and disappeared into the Light of God.

She felt her spirit slam back into her body again, on the sterile bed in that small room, still holding the lifeless hand of her son. Her eyes spilled over with tears of grief for herself and tears of joy for him, and she whispered back, "Thank you, Jared."

Oona went on from that loss to become a great spiritual inspiration to everyone around her, changing lives everywhere she goes as surely as her child changed hers, aware beyond any doubt that her ongoing work is proof of the purpose of the Mystical Traveler who ignited her faith and showed her the stars. He was here to touch and to teach, and he left when he'd accomplished exactly that.

To those who try to convince her that her experience at Jared's death was that tired old "grief-induced hallucination" cliché, she simply smiles, not needing to prove a thing to anyone, and offers her own paraphrase of a quote from another Mystical Traveler, Mattie Stepanek, who left this earth at the age of fourteen (and if you haven't read that extraordinary boy's books of poetry, run, don't walk, to your nearest bookstore): "Why not believe? It's a beautiful thing to believe."

———————

OF ALL THE countries I've visited, either privately or on my group excursions, I've never found a place more resistant to the mythical and paranormal worlds than the United States. Maybe it's because America is so young; maybe it will become more aware as it grows up. I don't know. But among its polar opposites in being comfortably in touch with other dimension are the British Isles, particularly Ireland.

I learned that lesson almost immediately upon my arrival in Dublin on a quasi-vacation. I was studying the menu in the cellar restaurant of the Merrian Hotel when I noticed a woman with short dark hair, wearing a maid's uniform. I made eye contact with her and she stepped right over to my table, warm and perky as could be.

"My name is Maryann Sullivan, and I'm glad you can see me," she chirped, and then promptly vanished into thin air as a waiter arrived.

"You know you have a ghost," I told him.

"Yes, we've all seen her," he replied with a pleasant smile. "Now, what may I bring you for dinner?"

Now, seriously, how refreshing is that? And that lovely, embracing lack of cynicism about other dimensions was apparent everywhere I went.

There was a dinner party at a friend's house at which a woman named Edna casually announced, "I have a ghost."

"Yes, you do," I said. "He's a Franciscan monk."

"How did you know?"

"I'm psychic." She accepted that without even a blink of hesitation, so I went on to tell her about her ghost. His name was John Fitzgerald, and he had fallen deeply in love with a local girl. He was so afraid he would betray his vow of celibacy in his passion for her that he hung himself, and he believed he would be doomed to an eternity in hell if he moved on from earth, so he's decided to stay right where he lived centuries ago.

There was no amazement, no eye rolling, no skepticism whatsoever as Edna listened intently to her ghost's story. When I finished she simply said, "Thank you, that's very helpful. I called for my vicar to come send the ghost on his way, but he wouldn't release him without knowing his name and his history. Now we can proceed. Well done, and thank you again."

A few days later it was on to the stunning ninth-century masterpiece called Ashford Castle in the west Ireland town of Cong. With the castle's massive entry doors, the moat, the breathtaking grounds, and the utterly impeccable decor, I felt as if I had stepped through a time warp into a long-past era in which I was not clomping around in my luggage-wrinkled pants, no makeup, and an artless blob of hair on top of my head. Instead, every minute of my stay in that castle made me feel as if I were gliding from room to room perfectly, exquisitely coiffed and groomed, in evening wear that Grace Kelly would have killed for.

I was invited to "take high tea in the drawing room," mind you, and settled into an antique wingback chair by the window beneath the largest, most awe-inspiring crystal chandelier I've ever seen. I was losing myself in the view of swans serenely floating on the glassy lake among the emerald-colored hills when I caught a flash of pink moving through the drawing room and looked toward it.

It was the pink chiffon nightdress of a beautiful woman with long golden hair. I psychically knew her name was Lady Arlington Humphreys, and she did nothing more than smile a little in my direction as she crossed through the room and out the door.

When the waitress arrived with my tea and scones I asked if she was aware that there was a ghost in the castle.

Again, nothing more or less than pleasant nonchalance. "Yes, there is. Did you see her?"

"She just walked by," I told her.

"Ah, yes. We see her almost every day, just around teatime." She finished serving me and left me to my tea, scones, and placid view.

Later, while walking through the foyer, exhausted and intending to go straight back to my room, I felt a strong energy pull coming from behind one of the many closed doors encircling the vast entryway. I followed it into a library that took my breath away. The walls were floor-to-ceiling gleaming wood shelves filled with a world of books. A seven-foot-tall fireplace was surrounded by comfortable red leather chairs. Marble floors were accented with rich Persian rugs. Just standing in the middle of that library was like letting out a deep, long overdue exhale, and I found myself wondering how long I could get away with living there without anyone noticing.

It took my eyes a few moments to adjust to the dimmed lighting. When they did, I noticed an elderly gentleman sitting in one of the overstuffed leather chairs. He had a full head of white hair with a hint of red running through it. His muttonchops were meticulously groomed, and his handlebar moustache was expertly waxed. He wore a red smoking jacket and a silk ascot. His legs were crossed, making it easier to see shoes shined so brilliantly that I was sure I could have seen myself in them if I were standing close enough. He held a book in one hand and a handkerchief in the other.

He completely ignored me, just kept on reading until suddenly he coughed a harsh, deep cough, covering his mouth with his handkerchief. When he lowered the handkerchief again I could see blood spots on the white monogrammed linen, and I realized that he'd died of tuberculosis. I wanted to talk to him and took a few slow steps toward him, but when I was a couple of feet away, he disappeared.

His name didn't come to me, nor did his story beyond the reason for his death. But the castle staff knew exactly who he was. "We see him all the time," a concierge told me. "He died here just as he was about to lose his castle. We think that's why he's so reluctant to leave."

————

WITHOUT A DOUBT the biggest joke on me in all my visits to Ireland happened during a charming horse-and-buggy ride around the Ring of Kerry. To fully appreciate this story, you need to understand that when I was a child, Grandma Ada loved to tell me about the fairies she used to see outside her family home near Hamburg, Germany. I was delighted to listen to everything she had to say, and I was delighted by the whole idea of fairies. From what I gathered in bits and pieces of the legends she told me, there were good fairies and bad fairies. They could be heroic, they could clean your house, and they could steal your baby. (I listened, but obviously not that closely.) They were tiny, with gossamer wings, and Grandma Ada's belief in their existence was absolute.

I never wanted to discourage her by admitting that I wasn't buying a single word she had to say about fairies, any more than I believed that giants live at the top of certain beanstalks, but I loved the stories, and I thought it was cute as a button of her to think they were real.

So there I was, a shameless tourist in Ireland, content and relaxed in this horse-drawn buggy, enchanted by everything from the land-scape to the tan plaid coat, newsboy cap, ancient face, and thick brogue of the driver. I lost myself in the incredible lush gardens we slowly trotted past, gaped at plants I never knew existed in shades of green I swear I'd never seen before, and looked up as we rounded a bend and came upon an oleander so gigantic that it looked like a movie prop.

And near its base, in a mottled patch of sunlight, there sat a fairy. An honest-to-God, my-apologies-to-Grandma-Ada, I-couldn't-have-been-more-wrong, living, breathing fairy.

She wasn't quite a foot tall. Her blond hair was tied into a bun on top of her head—yes, like Tinkerbell, what can I say? Her dress was shimmering green, her translucent wings fluttered in the passing breeze, and her head was tilted back a little, as if the sun felt good on her tiny, delicate face.

The only sound I could manage was a quiet gasp. Other than that, it was one of the few times in my life when I've found myself speech-less, and my mind was scrambling around trying to come up with some logical explanation, since, of course, there's no such thing as fairies—"I'm not really seeing this, it's probably jet lag, it's a mirage, if I drank I'd at least have an excuse for this," and finally, "Maybe if

I blink she'll be gone." I blinked. She wasn't gone. In fact, she stared back at me for a moment, nothing more than an acknowledgment that yes, she knew I could see her and she could see me too.

I'm not sure I was even aware of saying it out loud when I quietly erupted, "Dear God, I think I just saw a fairy."

The driver didn't bother to turn his head to reply, "So ye did, miss. They live all over this area."

"You're kidding," was all I could manage.

He turned, smiled, and gave me a wink. "Not to worry, miss," he said with quiet reassurance. "I saw her too."

You see, I really do understand why people have trouble believing in things I can see that they can't, and why I do wish each of you a visit from the afterlife, even if it's only once. There was no way around it; I came home from Ireland with lots of new ghost stories for the Nirvana Foundation and a belief in fairies as absolute as Grandma Ada's.

———————

IT WAS CLOSER to home that I learned a fascinating lesson in Looks Like a Haunting But Isn't. It explained more about what was happening in that awful Kansas City house Gary and I lived in before heading to California.

Dal and I were driving home to San Jose after a few days in Palm Springs. It was dusk when we got to a stretch of Highway 152 known as Pacheco Pass, which I'd heard of casually for no particular reason. I was staring mindlessly out the window when, with no warning, I was in the grip of sheer soul-shattering panic. It tore into me with such force that I was gasping to breathe. I had the immediate impulse to pray, but my head was so full of chaotic noises that I couldn't remember anything past "Our Father . . ." I heard screaming, cries of rage, violence, agony, and terror, and I thought that if there were such a thing as hell, it would sound like this.

Then the visions started, a parade of brutal images in quick flashes: a terrified child in a covered wagon surrounded by Indians; men in cloaks flogging Indians who were bound with chains; a corpse hanging from a tree; helpless families trapped inside wood cabins being ignited by flaming torches; and American and Mexican settlers firing at each other with long rifles. I closed my eyes to shut out the horror, but I could still smell a sickening combination of gunpowder, acrid smoke, and blood. Dal told me later that I grabbed his arm and screamed, "Help me!" but he was unable to pull over on the narrow road.

I have no idea how much time and how many miles passed before the psychic assault faded away, but the depression it left in my soul lasted for days. I'd never experienced anything like it in my life, and I couldn't imagine what it was, let alone what caused it. I was sure I couldn't possibly be the only person who'd gone through something devastating on that stretch of road, so I reached out through a local radio station and asked people to contact the Nirvana Foundation office if anything unusual had ever happened to them in Pacheco Pass.

We were immediately flooded with calls and letters, reporting everything from feelings of "desperate anticipation" and "truly believed my death was imminent" to a California Highway Patrol lieutenant who told me that Pacheco Pass was legendary in that part of the state. The above-average number of accidents, violent road rage incidents, and suicides led to a widespread law enforcement belief that "they're all trying to die quick up there," and he ended the conversation with, "I know people who drive miles out of their way to avoid Pacheco Pass because they're scared to death of it."

Several people noticed an inexplicable time distortion in the area. One letter described gaining forty-five minutes going one way through the pass and losing an hour coming back. That made me even more curious than frightened, which I would have bet wasn't possible, and I forced myself to drive through Pacheco Pass again with three of my researchers. We synchronized our watches and came up with the same results: on our round-trip through the pass, we lost an hour.

It was obviously time to see if the solution to this terrifying chaos could be found in the history of Pacheco Pass. The more I read the more apparent it became that the sounds, smells, and images that crashed into me that first day were consistent with the tragic past of the road cut into the mountain ranges between the inland Interstate 5 and Highway 101, the north-south freeway close to the California coastline.

Pacheco Pass was named for a landowner named Don Francisco Pacheco in 1843. The Spanish feudal lords who ruled the area at the time were so violently cruel to the American Indians who were chained, beaten, and killed as slaves that the road became known as the "Trail of Tears." Mexican bandits and Indians who'd escaped from slavery eventually waged war against each other, and American settlers who flocked to California during the Gold Rush later in the 1800s joined the fray.

The viciousness, grief, agony, and terror that took place on the land were so intensely concentrated that they became a very real, tangible part of the atmosphere itself, a phenomenon called an "imprint," as Francine explained to me. An imprint is an energy vortex, like an emotional version of the Bermuda Triangle, in which extreme feelings, positive or negative, accumulate in a specific area and become self-contained and self-sustaining as time goes on. The atmosphere in and around the area acts much like an invisible veil on which the energy imprints itself as the vortex continues to turn in on itself and intensify by feeding on any added energy that crosses its path. In other words, on my first trip through Pacheco Pass, I had an intense reaction to the atmosphere that was imprinted there, and my intense reaction fed and strengthened the imprint.

Now that I've researched imprints and understand how and why they can be distinguished from hauntings, I've found them to be great sources of fascination. I'm sure you have too when you've experienced them, whether the experiences came in the form of sounds, smells, and images or simply profound emotions. If you've ever found yourself terribly frightened, grief stricken, anxious, disoriented, or depressed during and after visiting battlefields, abandoned concentration camps and prisons, Ground Zero in New York, and other sites of obscene violence, you've felt the impact of an imprint. Imprints aren't always created by violence, though, as you know if you've ever been emotionally overwhelmed in the presence of the Wailing Wall or the Vietnam Memorial or Arlington National Cemetery, or if you've made the pilgrimage to Lourdes or Fatima or any of the other sites of sacred visions and healing miracles. There are great and small imprints all over the world; understanding what they are can keep you from feeling as if you're either under siege from something evil or just plain going insane—like, for example, if you're being terrorized in a trilevel suburban Kansas City house that happens to be sitting on top of an Indian burial ground.

I LEARNED YET another nuance of imprints on a trip to Kansas City with Paul and Chris. I decided I wanted them to see the wonderful house on Charlotte Street Daddy had bought for us when I was nine years old, a house I adored despite the sadness and turmoil that sometimes intruded on us there. Some of my most cherished, joyful memories with Daddy and with Grandma Ada took place in that house, and I was so happy to find as we pulled up to the curb that it was occupied, full of life, and beautifully cared for.

The current owner answered the doorbell. I apologized for the unexpected appearance of three strangers on her porch and started to introduce myself, but she interrupted. "I know exactly who you are," she said, warm and friendly. "You used to live here, didn't you? I hear that voice around here every day of my life."

I asked what she meant—it's not unusual for people to recognize my voice, but I couldn't imagine how she knew I'd lived there. She invited us inside while she explained that my voice and my laughter had been subtly drifting through the house since the day she moved in.

"I even know which bedroom was yours. Most of the laughter comes from there," she announced as she led us up the stairs.

She stopped and gestured toward the first bedroom on the right at the top of the stairway. My old bedroom. An awfully good guess, if that's what it was, in a sprawling four-bedroom house with downstairs rooms that could easily have been bedrooms as well.

She gave us the full tour, and it gave me such a wonderful sense of peace to know that this wonderful place was every bit as big and pretty and welcoming as I remembered it and that it was so obviously being appreciated.

As we sat down for the coffee she offered us, she chuckled a little and patted my hand. "I've never said this to anyone before, and I hope it comes out the way I mean it, but after all these years of feeling as if my family has been sharing this house with you, I'm pleasantly surprised to see that you're alive. I just assumed you were a ghost."

I took it exactly the way she meant it, and I was honestly surprised too. Most of the disembodied voices I'd experienced all my life were from the deceased, and the rest were the result of astral trips I've never been comfortable with unless I'm asleep. It sounded to me as if something else was going on. Sure enough, a lot of research and experience later, I've learned that all of us right here on earth can and do create imprints of our own in places where we've invested intense emotion, whether it's positive or negative. Now, on one hand, I love knowing that we have the ability to leave joy, laughter, and peace stamped into the atmosphere of places we leave behind without having to die to accomplish it. On the other hand, though, it's just as possible to stick the new tenants or owners with imprints of anger, violence, fear, sorrow, and a whole array of other negativity to deal with and add to through their reactions to it, which seems just plain irresponsible.

I hope you'll ask yourself the same question from time to time that I've asked myself ever since that lovely day in Kansas City: as you go about your daily business, at home, at the office, wherever you happen to find yourself: What kind of imprint are you leaving behind?

NINE

ANOTHER BEGINNING, ANOTHER ENDING

On April 12, 1986, while driving to a lecture, I decided to start a church. I'm sure the idea had been sneaking up on me for awhile, but when it snapped into focus, it felt exactly that sudden and so exciting that I blurted out the announcement to the two thousand people gathered in Cupertino, California, that day. My staff made supportive noises when I told them, although I wouldn't be surprised if they were thinking, "Yeah, that's really great, it only takes us eighteen hours a day to keep up with everything around here. We were wondering what to do with those other six hours." (It's a tribute to their tireless commitment that since that day, at their request, I've ordained many of them as ministers. For the most part, I've been the luckiest person on earth when it comes to my staff.)

Over the years, thanks to my studies of world religions, philosophy, and spirituality, I'd evolved into a Gnostic Christian. Without going into a long dissertation, and to grossly oversimplify it, Gnostic Christianity (from the Greek word *gnosis*, which means "knowledge") teaches that we all, as children of an all-loving, all-knowing, all-forgiving God, have access to an intimate relationship with Him, not through dogma and arbitrary rules so common to many religions but through intellect, understanding, and spiritual growth. It's inclusive rather than exclusive—there's none of this "Believe the way we do or you're going straight to hell" nonsense. It encourages thinking and holds that, although faith is essential, beliefs are at their deepest and most powerful when they make sense and answer more questions than they raise.

I created my church on the basic foundations of Gnostic Christianity and called it *Novus Spiritus*, or "New Spirit." It's a nondenominational, nonprofit organization whose commitment is to reach out to anyone who wants to deepen their faith, explore their soul's journey, uncover their highest purposes in this life, and find an alternative to the confusion or even feelings of rejection often caused by traditional religion.

Novus Spiritus doesn't tell you what to believe. We simply encourage open-minded learning and *thinking*, taking what you need, and leaving the rest behind. We open our arms to anyone and everyone, but we don't solicit converts. We're an active worldwide humanitarian organization, with ministers trained for everything from leading our prayer chains to conducting study groups and hypnosis sessions to working with local facilities for the homeless, the elderly, the physically and mentally challenged, battered women, and abused or neglected children.

We embrace a belief in reincarnation, which was an integral part of Christianity before the church was restructured under Pope Constantine in the sixth century. (Despite Constantine's best efforts, there is still a lot of biblical support for the concept of reincarnation.)

We embrace both male and female aspects of the deity—a Father God and a Mother God, called Azna, following a religious tradition that dates back more than twenty-five hundred years. She is the emotional dimension of the Godhead, while our Father is the intellect, and they are equal, inseparable, and mutually divine.

We believe in, worship, and celebrate God without fear, guilt, or punishment, or threats of Satan and/or hell, neither of which even exist. God is perfect, unwavering, loving, forgiving, compassionate. Vengeance, hatred, pettiness, ignorance, bigotry, anger, impatience, and retribution are traits that have nothing to do with God at all. Instead, they're human-made flaws, ours to overcome as the journey of our souls progresses. There is far greater joy in serving God, or anyone, for that matter, out of love than out of intimidation.

There are eighteen basic tenets of Novus Spiritus that form the basic, active guidelines on which I founded the church:

1. *The Way of All Peace.* This path scales the mountain of Self. By focusing energy outward toward others, and being of service, we can break through our self-imposed limitations of doubts, worries, and inhibitions.

2. *Love.* Love is a force, the perfect emanation of good as defined by God. No genuine love (that is, love devoid of selfishness, neediness, and/or ulterior motives) is ever lost. Put out into the world, it will be absorbed by someone or something that needs it, and it will always come back to you, whether you recognize it or not.

3. *Purity.* God is pure in Her/His love, while humans are erratic and subject to petty, dark behavior. Never ascribe pettiness or darkness to God, who is incapable of it. As for us, learning to choose Light over darkness is an important step on the path to the soul's perfection.

4. *Creator.* We are all a part of God, our Creator, just as we all carry the spark of the Divine within our souls, which means that each of us is born in possession of strength, goodness, and beauty that can make their mark on the world around us if we'll only tap into them.

5.   *Power.* Cultivating the spark of the Divine within us and recognizing it as a force at our disposal gives us the power of God moving on earth, especially when we turn that power outward to help others.

6.   *Faith.* Faith is our greatest tool. It gets us through the worst we have to endure when we have the faith to recognize God as our constant companion and turn to Her/Him for help. Faith is not just believing but knowing that we will never be asked to endure more than our souls can take.

7.   *Life.* Life is a journey during which we can learn from each step and misstep, better ourselves on the next step, and simply keep moving toward the greatest wisdom our spirits can achieve.

8.   *Judgment.* We can judge the acts of other people and be subjected to social laws ourselves, but we must never let any person claim to have dominion over our spirits. Only God is qualified to judge the soul.

9.   *Light.* Let the God-given beauty of your soul be a beacon for others in this dark world. Don't tell others how to live—*show* them, by your example of joy, purpose, compassion, and service.

10. *Growth.* Reach outward to grasp God, then find the God within yourself, and forge a bond between the two, living and actualizing this bond every day of your life.

11. *Communion.* Banish any thoughts of sin, devils, and demons. The only demons in this world are self-doubt, insecurity, and a fear that we're unworthy of God's love. Because we are all Her/His children, we're born with that love unconditionally—it's not withheld until we attain perfection.

Imagine how lonely God would be if that were the case.
As for sin, the only "sin" we commit is ultimately against
ourselves, since the only soul that's scarred when we willfully
and maliciously harm another living being is our own. The
soul ultimately seeks to make restitution with a loving God
for guidance, without the threat of nonexistent eternal
damnation.

12. *Divine.* The spark of the Divine in each one of us, the spark
we call our spirit or soul, is worthy of all the respect given
to God.

13. *Perfection.* God never inflicts pain on us. We chart it for
ourselves, for the growth of our souls, because without pain,
obstacles, and negativity we have nothing to overcome and
no way to learn and move closer to our own perfection.

14. *Karma.* Karma is simply a balance of experiences, both in
this life and from one life to the next. Each of us, with God's
guidance, selects our own balance, based on the advancement
of our souls and what we still need to learn.

15. *Reincarnation.* Each of us has many opportunities to live in
this world, and each life brings us closer to perfection until
eventually no further incarnations will be needed. The
true concept of being "saved" means reaching that level of
perfection ordained between us and God.

16. *Meaning of Life.* It's really as simple as this: Do good, love God,
then shut up and go Home.

17. *War.* Overt killing defiles the temple of God. However, when
attacked, it is compulsory to defend that temple.

18. *Death.* Death is the reward of living. It isn't to be feared. And
no matter how frightened we might be that damnation awaits

us, we can rest assured that there is no such thing—the grace
of God will counsel and heal us and give us another lifetime
to balance our souls.

It's an understatement to say that Francine is the cofounder of
Novus Spiritus. A huge percentage of the philosophies on which the
church is based originated in the thousands upon thousands of pages
of transcripts from my trance sessions with her; Novus Spiritus held
regular evening trance sessions in addition to our weekly church
services. One of the most remarkable sessions happened in our
small church near San Jose, where a capacity crowd of sixty people
had gathered with their tape recorders to listen to one of Francine's
lectures.

Francine was in the middle of her talk when she stopped and
focused on a woman who was seated near the front of the room.
The woman was holding a frail, shockingly thin little girl in her
lap. Francine looked into the woman's sad eyes and said, "Bring her
here."

The woman was weeping as she carried her child to Francine's
chair. You can hear on tape that her voice is so choked with tears
she can barely speak. "This is my daughter Anna, Francine. She's
only three, and she's dying of bone cancer. The chemotherapy isn't
helping, and the doctors say she's only got six more months to live.
I'm begging you, if there's anything you can do, please, please help
my child."

It never ceases to amaze me that no matter how heartbreaking the
issue at hand might be, Francine's voice never changes from her slow,
precise, emotionless monotone. By all accounts, everyone else in the
room was sobbing, while Francine simply and evenly commanded,
"Lay her across me. I will let my energy pass to her."

The woman gently placed the child in Francine's lap. Francine
closed her eyes. Her lips were moving, although no one but the little

girl could hear what she was saying. After a few minutes, Francine looked up at the woman again and said, "You can take her now."

Within a week Anna showed some signs of improvement. Within a month her doctors were mystified to discover that they couldn't find a trace of cancer in Anna's body. She's now in college and still sends occasional cards and photos to Francine, in care of me, as recently as my birthday.

———————

THAT STORY, MUCH like the Raheim story in chapter 6, is a great reminder of the exit points we've discussed. Both this child and the child Raheim healed had arrived at one of the exit points, or opportunities to go Home, that they designed into their charts. Neither Francine nor Raheim can interfere with a chart or make the ultimate decision for us about accepting or rejecting an exit point. That decision is strictly between each of us and God. These children clearly chose to reject their exit points and continue with their lives, and the powerful energy Francine and Raheim were able to pass along to them clearly gave them the cleansing, healing strength with which to recover. I made the same case about those healings of clients who come to me for readings: we're not interfering with or intervening in anyone's charts when they come to us. Their coming to me or Francine or Raheim in the first place means that, by definition, they charted those encounters, and we're simply holding up our end of what they already planned.

Not a day goes by that I'm not proud of and inspired by the ongoing work of Novus Spiritus. Since that brainstorm during a routine drive to a lecture in 1986, it's grown to four active churches, in Campbell, California; Renton, Washington; Allen Park, Michigan; and Las Vegas, Nevada. We have forty-five ministers and a membership of more than eight thousand. There are also organized study groups, which are essentially mini-parishes that meet every week or every month depending on the preferences of the members, to study and discuss church philosophies—five hundred study groups in the United States and fifty in other countries. It takes my breath away, and I'm so grateful.

ONE OF OUR first experiences on arriving back Home is a trip to the Scanning Machine, in a very sacred room in a magnificent building called the Hall of Wisdom. The Scanning Machine is a huge convex dome of blue glass in which we watch every minute of the lives we've just lived rerun before our eyes in a kind of three-dimensional hologram form—the good, the bad, the smart, the jaw-droppingly stupid, the kind, the cruel, you name it, we stand there and review it from start to finish, not so that God can judge how we did but so that we can judge it for ourselves with no interference from our human defense mechanisms. You've heard people who've had a close brush with death make the comment that their whole lives flashed before their eyes? They're not kidding. That simply means that they made it as far as the Scanning Machine before they chose to come back and take care of their unfinished business here on earth.

Maybe when I get to stand back and watch the next sequence of events that I charted for myself, it will make sense to me, because it sure stumps the hell out of me now.

IT WAS THE late 1980s. The Nirvana Foundation was thriving. Novus Spiritus was off to a thrilling start. I was averaging fifteen to twenty readings and/or regressive hypnosis sessions a day. I was enjoying regular television and radio appearances, and my lecture schedule was booked solid. So was my marriage falling apart just to keep me from getting spoiled? Was that the point?

Dal and I had long since settled into being much more like brother and sister than husband and wife. It wasn't ideal or especially stimulating, but it was okay, and worlds better than Gary's constant criticism, temper tantrums and unpredictable violence.

It seemed, though, that the busier and more gratifying my life became, the less involved Dal became and the more he withdrew into himself. I remember saying to someone at the time, "I thought Dal was a great conversationalist until I realized I was the one doing all the talking." "Quiet" probably wouldn't have bothered me all that much, but blatant disinterest, especially from a husband who was paying himself a respectable salary as my full-time business manager, was becoming unbearable. The sounds of video games coming from behind his closed office door became a source of incredulity among my perpetually busy staff, and at home he was such a silent, emotionally absent shadow that we spent a couple of years essentially separated but living in the same house. He'd also developed a variety of chronic health problems, especially with his back, his legs, and his blood pressure, and I was continually asking him if he was in pain and/or if he thought he might be suffering from depression. No. He was fine. As monosyllabically as possible. I admit it, a point came when I finally just stopped asking.

It's no big surprise, then, that I barely paid attention when he said something about a great business opportunity, recommended by some lawyer friend of his, a gold mine (literally), guaranteed investment, blah, blah. I had my hands more than full enough to involve myself with our finances, which were and had always been his responsibility, so while I had my reasons, I'll always regret that my only reply was, "As long as you don't touch a dime of the foundation's money or the Novus Spiritus funds, do whatever you want."

Not long after that we separated. Since it was at my insistence, I found an apartment for him and gave him what money I could

afford. He was so generally sedentary by then that Michael, a
member of my staff, had to physically move him out of the office
to make sure he wasn't still in his room months later, playing on his
computer without my noticing.

It was an energizing change for me, a little like being liberated
from the set of *Night of the Living Dead*. I continued to love every
aspect of my work, but now I also had the luxury of a home that felt
like a peaceful refuge rather than an endurance test. In the meantime, Michael and another loyal, longtime staff member, Larry Beck,
drove to Dal's supposed gold mine to check out his and my supposed "guaranteed investment." It was their opinion that there was
a whole lot more expensive equipment than gold to be found there
and no chance of salvaging however much of my money he'd poured
into it, especially since (ready?) Dal had apparently just thrown up
his hands and walked away from the whole thing. Again, as long as
the foundation and Novus Spiritus funds were safe, I'd work twenty-
four hours a day if I had to to make up for whatever Dal had cost
me. Michael and Larry did more than their part as well, even trying
unsuccessfully to sell tens of thousands of dollars worth of abandoned equipment. In fact, my whole staff was behind me a thousand
percent in whatever it took to put Dal behind me, and behind all of
us, once and for all.

That turned out to be a whole lot easier said than done.

First came the call from my lawyer, to tell me that Dal had been
arrested two weeks earlier. For fraud. I think I said something short-
sighted like, "Good. He probably deserves it."

Then came the hideous news that everything Dal had done, he'd
done with my name attached.

The SEC showed up in my office, wanting to discuss the fact that
Dal had publicly sold shares in that ridiculous gold mine, without
bothering to spring for the $25 or whatever it was for the license
that would have allowed him to sell them legally.

They were followed by the IRS, eager to collect on a staggering amount of taxes Dal had neglected to pay.

I paid back every dime the gold mine investors lost.

I accepted the IRS's gracious offer to set up a monthly payment plan and paid every dime of tax money owed.

I lost my house.

I lost my car.

I had no choice but to declare bankruptcy.

Never before or since have I been so devastated, so frightened, and more humiliated.

And of course the press had the time of their lives—what could be more fun than exposing the fact that a world-renowned psychic was involved in a fraud? The fact that my name was involved but I wasn't didn't seem to interest anyone but those closest to me, who'd seen it all unfold and knew I was guilty of nothing more and nothing less than not paying close enough attention and a serious case of misplaced trust. Frankly, if I'd read that claim under those circumstances, I wouldn't have believed me either. But at that point the truth seemed almost irrelevant. All I knew was that I was scared and embarrassed to my core, the reputation I'd spent nearly two decades working so hard to build had been carelessly and maybe fatally compromised. I was broke, and while I never wanted to leave my house ever again, I had to earn a living and somehow, in some way I couldn't begin to fathom, find the strength and the confidence to start over . . . again. . . .

MORE HELLOS,
MORE GOOD-BYES

It was 1990, and I had shifted into my usual crisis recovery mode—that is, staying so busy that I wouldn't have time to notice that I was feeling so shattered and frightened that I'd never find my way back to solid ground again. When a call came out of nowhere asking me to do a haunting investigation of the *Queen Mary* in the Long Beach, California, harbor for the Halloween episode of some new talk show, I said yes without even knowing or caring whose show it was or what the details were. I'd never been to the *Queen Mary* before and it sounded interesting, but far above and beyond that, I was in no position to turn down a paying job.

I arrived the day before the shoot, and that beautiful, historic ship really did take my breath away. It was vast, of course, filled with dark polished mahogany, gleaming brass railings, and massive crystal chandeliers, overall just a stunning trip back in time to the days when craftsmanship was a treasured art. I was glad I'd come early to get my sightseeing out of the way, although enchanted as I was with everything from the decor to the lovely dinner to my spacious cabin, I couldn't shake the uneasy awareness that there was an oppressiveness to the atmosphere. Or maybe it was me. I wasn't exactly a barrel of laughs at that point in time, and I was open to the possibility that I was bringing my own oppressiveness to this party.

I was exhausted, so I retired to my cabin right after dinner and fell into bed, appreciating the smells and sounds of the harbor outside my open porthole window for about three minutes, until word spread through the local mosquito community that I was in town and available for their dining and dancing pleasure. They swarmed around my cabin and me until it became unbearable, at which point I swatted my way to the porthole, slammed it shut, and fell back into bed. That's when I learned that there was a reason the porthole had been left open for my comfort—with it closed, the cabin instantly became sweltering hot and stifling, narrowing my choices down to either being eaten alive or being able to breathe. I opted for breathing, opened the porthole again, and settled back in to wallow in self-pity.

I was still wide awake, well past midnight, when I heard footsteps running up and down the hallway outside my cabin door. With a whole television crew on board the ship, footsteps weren't that big a surprise. But these sounded like suspiciously small feet for anyone I'd met on the crew, and there didn't seem to be any direction to the running back and forth. I crept to the door and opened it, very quietly.

A little boy ghost, filmy white and indistinct, was playfully darting around the hallway as if he were in the last few minutes of an imaginary soccer tournament. I couldn't make out any features other than a small frame wearing knickers and what looked like a newsboy cap. He didn't pay the slightest bit of attention to me, and he vanished before I could talk to him, so I scuffed back to bed, made room for myself among the mosquitoes, and eventually drifted off to sleep.

I was very sleepy, very cranky, and very itchy the next morning at breakfast when I told the production team about the little ghost boy in the hallway. They reacted with some combination of yawning and eye rolling. To be fair, it wasn't that great a story, and I had no way of proving I wasn't making it up, so I resigned myself to being thought of as the talk show's latest weirdo guest and headed off to shoot the on-camera tour.

"We'll start without our host," the producer told me. "He'll catch up with us shortly."

"Who cares?" I sneered silently to myself. I still didn't have a clue who our host was, so how excited was I supposed to be at the news that he'd be joining us shortly?

So off I went though the *Queen Mary*, audio and video technicians in tow, ready to capture every encounter with all the ghosts and spirits we met along the way. The problem was, there weren't any. From the gorgeous dining rooms to the ballroom, from one gleaming wood deck to another, from the guest cabins to the magnificent captain's quarters, there wasn't a hint of the afterlife aboard. Even the ghost boy from the night before seemed to have jumped ship, the little weasel. My mood was growing darker and darker as the bored-to-tears crew lumbered along in my wake, I'm sure wondering as I was if there was such a thing as an award for Lamest Halloween Talk Show Episode in Television History.

Our uneventful tour had gone on for what seemed like about seventeen years when we reached the lowest deck, where a swimming pool had once been. Words can't describe my shock and relief when suddenly a ghost, as distinct as the crew, materialized a few feet away from me. I froze in place, motioning for everyone else to stay where they were, and then stepped toward her.

She looked to be about twenty years old. She was all in white, from her mid-calf-length sleeveless party dress to the long strand of pearls around her neck to her opaque stockings to her low-heeled Mary Jane shoes. Her hair was in short, jet black finger waves, and her eyes were dark and dramatically lined with kohl. She was dancing, with her arms high in the air, and when I moved away from the crew she began twirling in circles around and around and around me. Her whirling dance was joyless, manic, and driven, and her wide smile seemed more deranged than happy.

As she spun past again, I asked, "What is your name?"

"Mary," she said. She didn't stop moving while she looked me over and then added, "You're dressed so oddly."

It was then that I noticed the angry red wounds on the inside of both her wrists, from what had obviously been a successful suicide attempt. I asked if the cuts hurt her.

"Not any more," she said, laughing. In the next breath her laughter turned to angry defensiveness. "And they're not cuts, they're just scratches."

I took another step toward her, keeping my voice quiet and calming. "No, they're deep cuts, Mary. Tell me what happened."

She never stopped her insane dance while she was talking, and her tragic story was interrupted with occasional giggling. There was a man named Robert. She was deeply in love with him, and they were engaged to be married. Then one day, with no warning, no apologies and not even a note, he ran off to marry a woman who was wealthier than she was. She was disconsolate, and her worried parents promptly booked passage for the three of them on the *Queen Mary* in the hope that an extended family trip to Europe might help mend her broken heart.

"This is our third day," she told me, and it was a safe guess that probably, on the third day of the cruise with her parents, she went to the lowest deck of the ship and slit her wrists. "And you know what's going to happen?"

"What's going to happen?"

Her voice was giddy and conspiratorial as she whirled by again and said, "He's going to leave her and come back to me. He'll wire me through the ship's captain and tell me he's waiting for me in England."

I needed to tell her that Robert was dead, and that she was dead, but she was so deeply disturbed that I knew I had to be gentle about breaking it to her. I began, "Mary, you can be with Robert right now if you'll let me help. . . ."

At that moment a hushed baritone voice behind me interrupted. "Who are you talking to?"

I turned around and looked into the handsome, sensitive face of a man I was sure must be our long-awaited host.

I held out my hand. "Sylvia Browne," I said.

"Montel Williams," he replied with a firm, confident handshake.

I know many of you have had the experience of meeting a total stranger and having to fight the urge to say, "Oh, *there* you are! I wondered when you were going to come into my life." When that happens, when a first meeting feels more like a reunion, you can count on it that the two of you charted each other.

Let this be a lesson to all of us: at an awful time in my life, after a miserable night, the last thing I was expecting was to meet someone who would make such a beautiful difference to me in so many ways for so very long. It's a great story to remember when occasional, inevitable feelings of hopelessness set in: there are nice surprises waiting for you somewhere, so just keep putting one foot in front of the other and hang in there.

He repeated, "Who are you talking to?" I snapped out of the impact of meeting him and got back to the subject at hand. I told him about Mary and her tragic story while he listened intently, not sure whether he was buying this or not but open minded enough and too good a host to laugh in my face.

"She's here right now?" he asked, looking around and seeing nothing. I nodded, and he added, "What's she doing?"

I told him that she'd now started twirling around both of us, and she was paying close attention to our conversation and enjoying the fact that we were talking about her. He was genuinely trying to see her, and while I knew I couldn't make that happen if he wasn't "tuned" that way, I was sure I could at least let him experience her if she would cooperate.

I asked Mary to stand still. She did. Then I took Montel's hand and, without a word, pulled him right into her ethereal body.

You've never seen such huge eyes in your life as his after he'd stepped through his very first ghost. He was clearly shaken, and the only words he could get out of his mouth were, "Oh, my God!"

"Did you feel that?" I asked, deliberately nonchalant.

"Feel it? How could I *not* feel it? Whatever it was, it was freezing cold. And not any kind of cold I've ever felt. It went all the way through me, right down to my bones. And just in that one spot you walked me through." He shuddered and added, "It was like walking through a wall of cobwebs, too. I can still feel them all over me."

I smiled, knowing from plenty of experience that the cobweb feeling would pass but the memory never would. All I said was, "So now you've met Mary."

He just nodded. Any skepticism he'd arrived with was gone now, not because I convinced him but because Mary did.

Mary, in the meantime, had lost interest in the conversation and whirled off into her own trapped world again. When we'd finished shooting, the show's producer excitedly told me that it was on this lower deck that the *Queen Mary* employees and guests had reported the majority of their paranormal experiences, from unexplainable noises to glimpses of something filmy white moving quickly past them. Now they knew why, and for those of you who've never visited that beautiful ocean liner, feel free to say hello to Mary on the lowest deck and try to send her Home. She's still there, and she could use your help.

Montel and I found a bench on the upper deck and sat down to talk. Twenty years later, we still haven't stopped.

THE PREVIOUS TWO years had been a relentless exercise in picking up the pieces and trying to rebuild my life from several paces behind square one. My family, friends, and staff had been wonderful, particularly Larry Beck, who'd been with me since the beginning of the Nirvana Foundation in 1974. He was a brilliant computer whiz, and he became an absolute warrior doing legal research and unraveling the many financial disasters Dal had created, working side by side with lawyers and accountants to minimize the damage as much as possible.

In fact, Larry, my longtime friend and assistant Linda Rossi, and I moved into an apartment together that was ideal in a lot of ways. It was affordable; it was in the same building as two more of my assistants, Michael and Ben; and best of all, we were able to move Daddy and Mother into an apartment just two doors away from mine. Both of them were having health struggles by now, so there would always be someone a few short steps away for anything they needed. And in the unlikely event that we weren't around, Sharon and Richard, who now had two sons, were living nearby as well; Sharon was still working for me.

Let's not forget Paul, who was now a successful mortgage broker. He and his wife Nancy and their brand-new son Jeffrey were very much around and supportive, as was Chris, who was doing a wonderful job of building his own well-deserved career as a psychic. He never left my side or let his grandparents need for a single thing, as generous and fiercely loyal as anyone I've ever known. When he met and married Gina, I think there was a long line of us watching her like a hawk, ready to run her over in a parking lot if she tried to take advantage of him, but in the end we all fell as much in love with her as he did.

I took every step I could think of to shove Dal firmly and completely behind me. I divorced him, of course. I also dissolved the

Nirvana Foundation, which he was part of from the very beginning, and formed the Sylvia Browne Corporation instead, adding an *e* to my last name to psychologically distinguish between Sylvia Brown, wife of Dal, and Sylvia Browne, rising from the ashes despite his hopelessly careless, fraudulent efforts to the contrary.

It took time, but finally that's what made it possible for me to forgive him—as horrible a mess as he'd made of my life, I never believed there was anything malicious in his intentions. Careless, irresponsible, lazy, incredibly foolish, yes. But not malicious. In the end, I was having a much tougher time forgiving myself for letting it happen and risking everything I'd worked so hard to build.

Thank God (and I mean that literally), the rest of the world seemed to be ready, willing, and eager to forgive me or unaware of what had happened in the first place. And I was so tired of dealing with it, being frightened about it, and crying myself to sleep about it that you can bet I wasn't about to bring it up.

Looking back, it's almost funny to remember the instant, frozen fear that crashed over me when, in the middle of a frantically busy day in 1993, I got a call from my old friend Ted Gunderson. I'm always happy to hear from old friends, but under the circumstances, since it was a call from an old friend *who's an FBI agent*, I had to stop myself from shrieking into the phone, "Whatever Dal's done now, I swear on my life I had nothing to do with it!"

I managed to keep my mouth shut, and when Ted explained why he was calling, I breathed a sigh of relief for myself and felt pretty sure that Dal was off the hook too. As everyone including me was sadly aware, on February 26, 1993, a Ryder truck had made its way to the underground parking garage of the World Trade Center's North Tower. At 12:17 p.m. fifteen hundred pounds of explosives inside the truck detonated. Six people were killed, more than a thousand were injured, and the American myth that terrorists would never strike here at home tragically began to crumble.

I'd worked with Ted on other cases, and my respect for him was and is unparalleled. Whatever I could do to help him, if I could help at all, no matter what, all he had to do was ask. By the time he called me, I'd read that three of the Islamic terrorist bombers had been arrested, and Ted wanted my psychic input on any others who might be involved.

I told him there were five, maybe six men involved, including the three in custody. On March 16, 1993, I was formally interviewed by the FBI on videotape. Excerpts of the tape have aired on national television, so public domain allows me to repeat a little of the transcript:

BROWNE: One of the men you need to look for has a short build . . . wiry . . . black hair . . . black eyebrows. . . . There's an "m" on there . . . S-a-l-z-e-m something . . . Salzeon . . . Salzemon . . . m-o-n. Okay, Salzemon.

A total of six Islamic terrorists were ultimately arrested by the FBI for the 1993 World Trade Center bombing. They were convicted in 1997 and 1998 and sentenced to an average of 240 years each for their crimes. One of the six was a short, wiry man with black hair and thick black eyebrows. His name was Mohammed A. Salameh. He'd been arrested on March 4, but his identity hadn't yet become public knowledge. No doubt about it, I was off by a few letters, but when Ted told me they'd arrested someone named Salameh, it was close enough that I screamed, "You got him!"

It was experiences like that, and the twenty readings a day I'd taken on, and the increasing success of Novus Spiritus, and continued referrals from the medical and psychiatric communities, and more appearances on Montel's show, and a lot of long talks with Francine that finally "relit my pilot light." Without knowing exactly when it happened, I went from just going through the motions to being passionate about my work again, and maybe even more committed than ever. From my incredible, loyal staff to my Novus Spiritus ministers to Chris to Larry to me, we all knocked ourselves out seven days a week. We could barely believe it when we realized we were getting back on our collective feet again, but we didn't doubt for a moment that we'd earned it.

———————

ONE APRIL MORNING in 1995 we were all in our respective offices, fielding a typically insane flood of phone calls, when we heard Larry yelling at the top of his lungs from behind his closed door, "Are you crazy?! Hang up and call an ambulance, for God's sake!" A second later he came racing out, grabbed me and pulled me toward the door. "That was Richard," he said. "He and Sharon just tried to wake your father up, but he's unconscious. Let's go."

I was too shocked and numb to remember much about the next few hours or days. Daddy, who'd been suffering for quite some time with a variety of serious illnesses including kidney cancer, was in a coma when he arrived at Valley Medical. He spent the next five days in intensive care. I spent the next five days at his bedside. On the fifth day, I left his room to stretch my legs and get a drink of water. I was gone for less than three minutes. And in those three minutes, Daddy died.

There just aren't words for that depth of grief, as those of you know who've been through it, and mine was compounded by the idiotic, irretrievable fact that I'd chosen those few moments to be away from him. How could I, of all people, not have been there to hold his hand and wish him a quick, joyful trip Home? Spiritually, I knew perfectly well that it was completely beside the point, that after a lifetime of such great love and in the context of the eternity he and I would be spending together, there was no unfinished business between us, and where I was for the last breath his body took was the height of trivia. Emotionally, it took me years to catch up with my spirituality and let go of that stupid drink of water that could so easily have waited.

It was eight months before I got a brief visit from Daddy. It started with a faint whiff of his signature cherry blend pipe tobacco. Then I saw him, just for a moment, sitting in his favorite chair, looking healthy, happy, and content.

It seemed like I'd been without him for a thousand years. "Daddy," I said, ecstatic, "what took you so long?"

"What do you mean? I just left."

See what I mean? Compared to the eternity that's the only measurement of time on the Other Side, eight months is the blink of an eye.

Then he was gone again. I still miss him and talk to him every single day. I know he's back to his busy, blissful life at Home. I know he hears me, and I know he's around me. But psychic or not, it's no comparison to having him here. It bears repeating: grief is nothing if not selfish.

I'm sure it was predictable, but I didn't see it coming—four months after Daddy died, in August 1995, Mother passed away from pneumonia. Daddy suffered for five long, excruciating days before he left. Mother was gone in just a few short hours. That didn't necessarily make sense to me, but it's not mine to figure out.

This might be a perfect time to mention Option Lines. You know those charts I keep mentioning that we write before we come here? Another aspect we design when we write them is a hand-selected area of our upcoming lives that we just can't seem to master no matter how hard we try or how well everything else seems to be going. That continually challenging part of our lives is called an Option Line, and we have seven possibilities to choose from when we write our charts:

1. Health
2. Spirituality
3. Love
4. Social life
5. Finances
6. Career
7. Family

See? You thought it was just you, didn't you? But when one of those seven essential elements of a well-balanced life is in continual turmoil, you can try to avoid it, you can try to conquer it, you can try burying yourself in denial and tell yourself everything's fine and/or it doesn't matter. The bottom line, though, is that because it's the Option Line you chose, it will always challenge you and always affect you.

Here's a surprise: I chose family.

Meanwhile, back at the office, Larry became my manager, professionally and financially. He'd gained my complete trust in our two decades together, and he'd been my knight in shining armor when I was at the lowest point in my life. He was as tireless and hard working as I was; there was nothing he didn't know about me, my business, and my priorities, no area of my life in which he wasn't involved; and living with him and Linda felt comfortable, safe, and solid, especially after Daddy and Mother passed away.

Larry asked me to marry him.

I couldn't imagine how I could possibly say no.

Our wedding and reception were at the Oddfellows Hall in San Jose, on September 9, 1996. I wore a white suit, and Larry wore a tuxedo. Chris walked me down the aisle, and all my ministers were there, along with what seemed like hundreds of friends and colleagues. Larry cried his eyes out from the beginning to the end of the ceremony. Reactions to that ranged from, "Isn't that sweet?" to, "What's wrong with him?"

Stealing the show, though, was the person Larry always called "Sylvia's heart on two legs": my extraordinary, brilliant, beautiful granddaughter, Chris and Gina's daughter Angelia ("Eya") Dufresne. She was three years old at the time and tiny, with black hair and violet eyes. She was our flower girl. She wore a shimmering green silk dress with pink bows, white stockings, and white Mary Jane shoes, and she looked and felt like a princess. The rehearsal the night before went perfectly, with Eya carefully dropping a few petals at a time from a little ribbon-draped basket as she slowly made her way up the aisle. The day of the wedding, however, she'd clearly become disenchanted with her assigned chore and/or, Scorpio that she is, decided it was stupid, because instead she marched up the aisle, got about three feet from the altar, dumped her basket of petals in the middle of the aisle, and then walked off to the side and put her hands on her hips. The unspoken statement was, "There. You wanted the petals out of the basket, the petals are out of the basket. Now what?" Stepping over that pile of rose petals when I arrived at the altar was probably my favorite moment in any of my three weddings.

Chris had bought a condo in Sunnyvale, and his wedding gift to Larry and me was the key to that condo.

The newlyweds Sylvia Browne and Larry Beck hit the ground running. (Keeping the name I already had was nonnegotiable. Let's face it, Sylvia Celeste Shoemaker Dufresne Brown Browne Beck is almost as exhausting to say as it was to accumulate.) I felt safe. Someone who'd proven himself to be on my side had committed to watching out for me from now on. My mind finally unclenched from the fear and the grief I'd been living with, and I was even working my way toward forgiving myself for the stupidity that had jeopardized so much of what mattered to me. With Larry in charge of the finances for me, the corporation, and Novus Spiritus so that I wasn't also preoccupied twenty-four hours a day with the expanding payroll, taxes, and the ongoing aftermath of my bankruptcy, I was, as the saying goes, ready to rock and roll again.

My first book had come out, and I was developing a productive relationship with its publisher Hay House. They were big believers in promoting their authors, and I was a big believer in saying yes to new opportunities, so we were remarkably compatible. Next thing I knew I was taking groups on spiritual cruises and junkets to places like the Caribbean, Greece, and Egypt, in addition to lecture tours throughout the United States and Canada. Montel Williams started inviting me back to his show on a regular basis. Larry King called, radio and cable shows called, and I found myself on all the network morning shows discussing everything from current criminal cases to political and celebrity predictions. The only shows I turned down were those that would have breached an unwritten handshake agreement between Montel and me in which I promised that I wouldn't appear on any other daytime talk show but his—in other words, I would be as loyal to him as he'd been to me since the day we met. While my ministers and staff were traveling around the country creating study groups and doing regressive hypnosis seminars, my client list—in person, through letters, and on the phone—was expanding, and my waiting list grew from months into years. To this day I appreciate and regret this at the same time—believe me, it's an enormous frustration when my staff tell clients I'll be getting back to them at 11:00 A.M. four years from Tuesday. In an effort to service more clients at once, I initiated groups called salons, in which I spend an afternoon, often joined by Francine, with twenty-five to fifty people for discussions, questions and answers, and spiritual exercises. During all that, I accepted a lecture tour offer from the Learning Annex that often took me to fifty or sixty cities a year. And since it's impossible to do readings while I'm touring, my waiting list kept growing while Novus Spiritus kept expanding, and above all I was determined to devote time to my family, which had also joyfully expanded: Angelia's little brother Willy was born and immediately had us all in the palm of his tiny, perpetually happy hand. By now Paul and Nancy and their son Jeffrey, and Chris and Gina and Angelia and Willy all lived close enough to Larry and me in our new house on a hill in San Jose that we were finally able to be vital parts of each other's lives, and I cherished every minute of it.

———

IN FACT, WILLY provided me with one of the more memorable moments in my years with the Learning Annex. It was already an emotional evening for me—for the first time, I was speaking at the legendary Palladium in the heart of Hollywood, a place Daddy and I had read about a thousand times in movie magazines. It had opened in 1940, and its first headliner was Frank Sinatra with the Tommy Dorsey Orchestra. From then on it seemed as if anyone who was anyone performed there; through the eyes of a couple of movie magazine junkies in Kansas City, it took on a certain Mecca quality. So when I walked out on the stage of that art deco treasure to a warm welcome from four thousand people, I had the rare experience of finding myself emotionally overwhelmed. I can count on less than one hand the number of times I've cried in public, but that night, very briefly, I couldn't help myself.

When the audience was quiet again I managed to find my voice. "My daddy used to say about this place, 'Sylvia, when you play the Palladium, you know you've made it.'" I picked up my water glass and raised it high in the air and, from the bottom of my heart, added, "This one's for you, Daddy."

God bless that audience, they applauded for several minutes, giving me a chance to walk from the podium to the wingback chair that was waiting for me in the middle of the stage and collect myself. I had an outline in mind for that night's lecture, but I felt Daddy's presence so strongly in that magical place, and missed him so intensely, that I launched into an impassioned, extemporaneous discussion about the death of a loved one, and the pain of grief, and how even when you know beyond all doubt that your loved one is still right there with you, there are moments when you feel as if you would sell your soul for just one more hug. . . .

In the midst of my heartfelt talk, the four thousand people in the audience began snickering, which grew to chuckling, which grew to gales of laughter, all in the course of a few seconds. I've never been more confused in my life. I was pouring my heart out, almost moving myself to tears, and they were finding it paralyzingly funny? And the laughter was so loud and so silly that I started wondering if maybe somehow my panties had fallen down around my ankles or there was a Bugs Bunny cartoon running on a screen behind me.

I turned to look, on the off chance I was right about the Bugs Bunny thing, and I immediately started laughing too. My precious grandson Willy, not quite three years old at the time, had wandered away from Chris and Gina backstage and casually strolled onstage, headed toward me as nonchalantly as if we were at home in my family room. In his left hand he was holding a half-eaten bagel. With his other hand he was demonstrating his latest discovery: his right index finger fit with uncanny perfection into his right nostril. He was successfully ignoring his father, who was racing around in front of the stage, arms extended, trying to convince Willy to come to him without calling at-tention to himself (as if that was a possibility). Instead Willy kept right on ambling to my chair, lit up like a little Christmas tree when we made eye contact, and through a mouthful of bagel offered a joyful, "Hi, Bagdah!" as if we hadn't seen each other in weeks. I was laughing harder than anyone else in the Palladium as I picked him up, smoth-ered him with kisses, and handed him down to his mortified father.

So much for getting a swelled head about my debut at an historic Hollywood icon. To this day I still run into people who were there that night, and they can't pass a simple quiz on what I had to say in the two hours we spent together, but they've never stopped enjoying their memories of Willy's three minutes onstage.

Not long after that night I was feeling lonely for Daddy and retrieved my favorite picture of him, just to stare at it for awhile and smile and cry over it as I still do from time to time. Willy crawled up on the sofa beside me, pointed to the framed photo, and asked, "Who that, Bagdah?"

I told him it was my father, his great-grandfather, who had to go Home before Willy got here but I knew they would have been the best of pals.

He studied Daddy's face for several seconds. And then, I swear to you, he looked up at me, gave me a grin and a playful wink and said, clear as a bell, "That's my girl."

In the first chapter of this book, when I wrote about my father, I mentioned the special wink and "That's my girl" that was his shorthand throughout my life for, "I adore you, I'm proud of you and no one else on earth is as special to me as you are."

No one else had ever said, "That's my girl," to me, and I can promise you that my two-and-a-half-year-old grandson had never said it to anyone in his life, let alone his Bagdah. I'm not even sure he knew what it meant. But I tell you what I am sure of: like every other child, Willy was so tuned in to the spirit world of the Home he had so recently come from that Daddy was easily able to channel that special message to me through that equally special little messenger.

Within a few short minutes Willy was back to playing with his fleet of toy trucks on the family room floor without another thought to the magical gift he'd just given me. I, on the other hand, will remember it for the rest of this lifetime and long after that.

ONE SUNDAY MORNING in October 1998 I called my fifth client of the day to do a reading. Her mother had given it to her as a birthday gift months earlier in the hope of cheering her up during a rough time in her life, and through some unheard-of set of circumstances I can't recall, I was able to work her in much sooner than usual. I can't recall the specifics of the reading—I rarely can, by the way, so please don't take it personally if we run into each other and I seem vague about what I might have told you a year (or two, or ten) earlier. What I can recall is that, while we'd definitely never met before, during the reading there seemed to be something familiar about her, or maybe I just related to her more than usual.

Chris had bought a condo for me in Los Angeles, and I held a salon there on a Saturday and Sunday in January 1999. This client from the reading in October, who happened to live in Los Angeles, came to that salon. It was a little like that moment when I first met Montel—she walked into the room and, laying eyes on each other for the first time, we each had one of those "There you are!" experiences. When she left at the end of Sunday's session I did something I'd never done before and have never done again—I slipped a note into her hand with my private phone number and the simple statement that I'd like us to be friends.

Her name was Lindsay Harrison. She'd been in Los Angeles since 1970, and a television and film writer since 1983, but she was born and raised in Osceola, Iowa, a three-hour drive from Kansas City. As we began spending whatever time together we could—considering our respectively loony schedules—we discovered that we were very much alike in a lot of ways, with very similar senses of humor and that basic midwestern practical, no-nonsense, strong work ethic approach to life. She'd be the first to say that she's not psychic, but she's not new to the paranormal, and a hand-in-hand relationship between Christianity and spirituality seems utterly logical to her.

We were at dinner a few months after the salon when I turned to her and said, "Let's write a book together." She gave me a whole list of reasons why that wasn't a good idea: she knew a lot about writing scripts but nothing about writing books; I was famous enough to find a well-known co-author whom publishers would get excited about; I deserved an experienced co-author, and she was sure that between her and her literary agent we could find the perfect one. . . .

I cut her off with a simple, "Well, I'm psychic, and you're it, so give it up."

Our first book, *The Other Side and Back*, was released in July 2000 and became a #1 *New York Times* bestseller. The book you're reading now is our fourteenth book. She and I have been through pretty much everything together, and we're both very grateful that we charted each other and that I had the psychic impulse to insist she write with me and refuse to let her talk me into finding someone else.

Through the Learning Annex I met a literary agent named Bonnie Solow, who had years of experience with the publishing industry. Bonnie sold our first book proposal to Dutton for a very generous advance. It looked as if Lindsay and I were both on our way to a whole new facet of our respective careers, and there was great rejoicing in the land . . . by everyone but Larry.

I'D ESSENTIALLY SEEN Larry every day of my life since the early 1970s when he joined the staff of the Nirvana Foundation, and I would have bet I knew him as well as I knew my own family. To this day I believe I did, until he married me, and it brought out the worst in him. And I was so used to him, and so grateful to him for all he'd done for me, that it took me awhile to notice.

One school of thought is that (hear me out) by marrying the "queen," Larry had anointed himself king. I hope that description gives you the general idea, because it's hard for me to say with a straight face. Despite years of alternating between begging and threats, I can't for the life of me get my staff and ministers to call me "your majesty." A few of them call me Mom, but that's as close as they've ever come.

Larry, on the other hand, immediately began greeting the office staff every day with a smug, "Good morning, slaves." Incredibly, he wasn't kidding. He'd worked side by side with most of them for decades, but suddenly, "Good morning, slaves"? My clients and lecture audiences became, but never to their faces, "supplicants." He had something condescending to say either to or about pretty much everyone in my life, and he once referred to himself in a private conversation with a friend as "superior." You know those people who use arrogance and a sense of entitlement as a cover for deep-seated feelings of insecurity? Larry wasn't one of those people. He proclaimed his superiority, and he meant it.

The other school of thought is that by marrying me, he came to believe he *was* me. He felt perfectly entitled (there's that word again, one of my major pet peeves) to sign my name to everything from personal letters to my driver's license renewal without my knowing a thing about it. (Imagine my glee when the Department of Motor Vehicles requested the pleasure of my company in person after noticing that the signature on my renewal bore no resemblance to any of my other signatures they had on file.) I'm sure I'll never know how many phone calls he made and took on my behalf without mentioning a word about them to me—in fact, he gave me a stern scolding one day for calling my publisher, whom I also considered a friend, "behind his back." And then there was the afternoon when two lovely reporters from the BBC came to the condo to interview me for an upcoming documentary. While discussing my philosophies about reincarnation, one of them asked me my feelings about transmutation (changing species from one incarnation to the next). Before

I could even open my mouth, Larry chimed right in with an authoritative, "Oh, we don't believe in transmutation." Now, that happens to be true, but I wish you could have seen those women's faces as they slowly turned to stare at him with identical looks of, "Who *are* you?"

Whichever school of thought was more accurate, or even if the correct answer is "Both," I can honestly say I'd stopped taking his abrasiveness seriously years earlier, and I couldn't really imagine anyone else taking him all that seriously either. Seven or eight hundred times a day he would say or do something outrageous, but I would tell him to shut up and brush it off and we'd go right on with whatever we were doing. He'd been good to me, and loyal; he'd devoted his life to me; he worked hard at totally managing every aspect of the offices and my finances; he fielded and coordinated offers for television, radio, and personal appearances; and his computer expertise was invaluable. If he tended to rub people the wrong way, and if he demanded a lot of attention (positive or negative) and a lot of control, at least he made up for it in other ways. I thought.

When the first serious "Uh oh" happened, it seemed to come out of left field, although I'm sure it shouldn't have. Angelia and I were having a great time working on a project on the little sewing machine I kept for her at my house, where she also had her own bedroom and enough of her beloved arts and crafts supplies to open her own store. We were both caught completely off guard when Larry came marching into the room, his face red with anger, steam practically spouting out the top of his head. And in front of that little girl, he began berating me for all the time and energy I'd been devoting to Chris and Angelia (or, to put it another way, my son and granddaughter) and, in the process, neglecting him.

Needless to say, I took him to the other end of the house, out of Eya's earshot, to finish that conversation. It didn't take long. I just clarified for him that neither he nor anyone else on earth was ever going to be more important to me than my children and grandchildren, or come between us, or dictate to me how much of my time and energy I spent on them. He could accept that and stay, or he could leave. Those were his only two options.

He stayed. I don't know that he ever accepted that fact of my life. It was more as if he tolerated it. He never made the mistake again of squaring off with me about it, but it wasn't my imagination that there was an edge in his voice from then on whenever he referred to Angelia as "Sylvia's heart on two legs."

———

SO LOOKING BACK, it's no big surprise that Larry wasn't celebrating when I signed with Bonnie Solow and she sold *The Other Side and Back* to Dutton. Even though he didn't know the first thing about the publishing business, Larry saw no reason why "we" should pay an agent when, as far as he was concerned, he was smarter than anyone I could possibly hire and handle negotiations brilliantly, thank you. A lot of the credit for the success my books have enjoyed goes to my dear Montel. As *The Montel Williams Show* became more and more of a daytime hit, I became a more and more frequent guest, and not once did he fail to hold up a copy of my latest book and promote it as if it were his own. During all these years we've shared more joys and sorrows than I can count, and I can't imagine my life without him— he's one of those aspects of my chart that I've never once scratched my head over.

———

MONTEL WAS ALSO partially responsible for the scariest experience of my life. It had nothing to do with ghosts, or near-death experiences, or anything even remotely related to the paranormal.

Believe it or not, the scariest experience of my life was my first live-telecast pay-per-view. It was produced by Hay House, and Montel personally invested a breathtaking amount of money in it as well. From the moment I signed the contracts committing to it, I was terrified, and not even all my prayers to Father God and Azna and long talks with Francine could calm me down. It didn't matter that I'd been on television a thousand or so times by then. This was going to be live, with no editing, no retakes, no comfortable host guiding the show, my first experience working without a net. In the weeks leading up to it I couldn't eat, I could barely sleep, and what sleep I did get was filled with nightmares ranging from no one watching, to row after row of empty audience seats, to falling flat on my face as I walked onstage, to my mind going so completely blank on camera that I stood there staring wordlessly into space while the audience began to boo as they filed out of the studio—you name it, I dreamed about it and panicked over it. A major part of my fear, I know, was the fact that Montel had invested in it so generously, and if I told him once I told him fifty times before it aired that if he lost a single dime of that investment, I would find a way to repay him if it took me the rest of my life.

As often happens when we work ourselves into a hopeless frenzy anticipating something, my first pay-per-view went beautifully, and once I settled into a rhythm with it, I had a great time. Montel made his money back, no one booed or walked out of the studio, I didn't trip and fall flat on my face even once, and it was successful enough that I was asked to do another one. I leapt at it, looked forward to it, and loved it.

Don't you sometimes wish you had back all the hours you spent worrying so that you could find something useful to do with them instead?

I REMEMBER THE early 2000s as a blur in a lot of ways. Between visiting my churches, Learning Annex appearances, book signings, *Montel* tapings and occasional *Larry King* shows, it wasn't unusual for me to travel to more than sixty cities a year, not including the group cruises and trips all over the world. Being home in San Jose meant family time, a full schedule of readings, hypnosis sessions, salons, radio shows, Novus Spiritus services, and always, always writing. I was also busily adding to my family, starting with a Golden Retriever and following with a Bichon, a West Highland Terrier, a Labradoodle, a Shih-tzu, a Pug, a Shar-Pei. The only real challenge about having pets is trying to give them a fraction of the love and joy they give us.

Those were satisfying, exhausting, stimulating years, one of those periods of my life when I know I couldn't have worked harder. In fact, I was so busy that when Larry announced one night on the way home from a sold-out lecture, "I've taken you as far as I can take you," I didn't recognize it as the red flag it was and only gave him the same stare those two women from the BBC had given him, the incredulous stare that asks, "Who *are* you?"

ELEVEN

HOW LONG HAS THIS BEEN GOING ON?

We were on a flight home from our second Egypt tour. It was September 3, 2001. I was reading, tired, appreciating the peace and quiet of the plane, looking forward to sleeping in my own bed again.

Larry turned to me and simply said, "I want a divorce."

I didn't see it coming, and it shocked me. But I'd be damned if I was going to let him see that. So all I said was, "Fine."

I found out later that I was the only person on the trip who hadn't seen it coming. It seems that at every opportunity, all over Egypt, while I was busy with our group, Larry and a woman I'll call S. had been disappearing for a few minutes or hours. And they'd decided they belonged together.

In retrospect, I couldn't agree more.

Not that he bothered to tell me about S. at the time. A flat, unemotional, "I want a divorce," was the best he could do.

S. had been part of the group on our first trip to Egypt the year before. She and Larry had been e-mailing each other ever since and apparently developing quite a bond. Again, color me clueless. I have to say, even if I had the slightest idea how to use a computer, it would never have occurred to me to check up on Larry's e-mail activities. Possibly because I'm so private myself, I've never been a snoop, particularly on the men in my life. The day won't come when I'll go through someone else's mail, or check the numbers on someone else's cell phone bill, or root around in someone else's drawers and papers. I'm not interested in being a parent, or a warden, when I'm in a relationship. For one thing, if it takes diligent supervision to keep a man around, I don't want anything to do with him. For another thing, I have far more productive things to do with my time.

So, who knows how many e-mails and God knows what else later, off we went on the second Egypt trip—me, Larry, and a lovely group of people that just happened to include S. I even thought it was nice that she'd enjoyed the first trip enough to come again. Duh.

An even bigger duh: Larry and I threw a party at the condo in Los Angeles for a few close friends and a handful of those from our Egypt group. Yes, S. was among the eight or ten guests. Very classy, don't you think, to accept the hospitality of a woman whose husband you've been developing a relationship with behind her back?

Make no mistake about it, though, once I finally started finding out about the relationship, my rage was aimed right between Larry's eyes. S. wasn't the one who'd made a commitment to me, after all. Larry had. I'd invested absolute trust in him, based on his decades of loyalty and his heroism when the whole Dal disaster hit the fan.

Did I love him? No.

Did the betrayal of the whole situation devastate me? You bet. In a way, it was far more painful than the end of Dal and me. What Dal did was many things, but it wasn't deliberately hurtful. What Larry did was. Intentions count as much as the acts themselves when it comes to karma as far as I'm concerned.

He was eager to head off to the Midwest and start his new life with S., and I was even more eager for him to go. (I take a firm

"There's the door" position on this kind of thing.) He informed me, though, that he would fly back every Wednesday to take care of the finances.

My answer to that: "Like hell you will."

The divorce was like most divorces—necessary, long, and unpleasant.

Because I had been his sole means of support since the 1970s, and he'd paid himself a very generous salary during our marriage, he was only too happy to accept the alimony the courts awarded him. Bless his heart.

From what I hear, he and S. are still in the Midwest. He's converted to her chosen religion of Hinduism. (They do believe in transmutation, by the way.) In the most recent photo I saw of him, he was wearing a turban.

I don't wish him ill.

PICKING UP THE pieces was getting to be a habit. I didn't enjoy it. I was hurt, and I was angry, but I'd obviously been through it before and I knew I'd get through it this time. Larry didn't exactly have a legion of fans, so it wasn't as if anyone around me was encouraging me to hang in there and hope for a reconciliation. In fact, I continued to hear Larry stories for years from a staggering number of people who apologized for not speaking up sooner but hadn't wanted to upset me. The only person my heart hurt for was my precious little grandson Willy. He and Larry had been good buddies, and Willy was too young to understand where his Poppy had gone. But we got him through it with a lot of extra love and attention and reassurance that none of the rest of us was going anywhere, no matter what, and before long he was back to his God-given sweet, happy self.

Despite Larry's assertion that he'd taken me as far as he could take me (pause for a brief eye roll), my life and work didn't miss a beat.

If anything, I became busier than ever and, oddly, more peaceful at
the same time. I hadn't realized until Larry was gone how constantly
pressured I'd been feeling to always do more and more and more.
I could never argue with his perpetual reminders that we needed
money and that I was behind on my readings, writing, correspon-
dence, phone list, you name it, but it led to a nagging sense of guilt,
and of letting down the seventy people on my payroll, when I'd take
a nap, or spend an evening relaxing with my family and/or friends, or
go to bed with the flu. It was a great relief to discover that, with no
one around to abrasively push me, I was twice as productive in half
the time and enjoying it twice as much. I knew for sure that I wasn't
just going to be fine, I was going to be better than ever.

Another thing I knew for sure: I was done with relationships
and marriage. Period. Not interested, not available, no thanks,
buh-bye.

———

I WAS SITTING in my office one day, minding my own business (or,
okay, it might have been someone else's), when I looked up to see
Dal Brown standing in the reception area. It had been almost fifteen
years since I'd seen him, and it was shocking, not just because it was
such a surprise but because he didn't look at all well. After a couple
of awkward moments, we walked back into my office and sat down.

Life hadn't been particularly kind to Dal since the ugly end of our
marriage. He'd been married and divorced again. He'd had a job
that he couldn't keep because his health was deteriorating. He had
no insurance, he'd been living in a motel, and he was broke.

I admit it, if I'd fantasized about this scenario, I might have
guessed that I would take a little perverse pleasure in hearing that
Dal's life had fallen apart without me. In real life, I took no pleasure
in it at all. Instead, it made me sad, and my heart went out to him.

So . . .

(Don't panic, this isn't going where you think it is.)

I moved him into my very roomy house and saw to it that he got the medical help he needed without the added stress of wondering where his next meal or clean shirt was coming from.

There was no reconciliation, no rekindling, no rushing into each other's arms in the hallway on some dark, lonely night. Absolutely not, *nada:* that ship had sailed so long ago and so irretrievably that it wasn't even a passing thought. I was doing for him what I knew was right and compassionate and what I knew I couldn't live with myself for not doing. He was appreciative and as helpful as his health would allow, and I have to say it was nice to feel at peace about him and remember that at one point in time we liked each other.

ONE OF THE happiest, most unexpected calls of my life came in September 2006, inviting me to appear as myself on three episodes of the Rolls-Royce of soap operas, *The Young and The Restless.* I strongly suspect the idea came from some interoffice whispering between the legendary Jeanne Cooper, whom I'd met a few months earlier at Lindsay's house, and the show's associate producer Josh O'Connell. However it happened, I warned them that scripted television isn't my forte, and they didn't care, so I was booked and looking forward to it.

In the script, I was conducting a séance in Katherine Chancellor's (Jeanne Cooper) mansion to help Katherine and her (supposed) daughter Jill Abbott (Jess Walton) find Jill's biological son, whom Katherine believed she had given away in a jealous alcoholic rage when he was an infant because the baby's father was Katherine's husband at the time. (Got it?) Because it was my séance, I had a million lines to memorize, which involves brain muscles that I'm not accustomed to using. It was hard work—in fact, I thought more than once, "These people do this every week, fifty-two weeks a year, and I think *I* work hard?"

I have to say: there are no nicer, more supportive, more compassionate people than that cast and crew of *The Young and the Restless*, and the queen of them all was Jeanne Cooper. From the moment I arrived, she took me under her wing and personally saw to it that I was welcomed, embraced, comfortable, and attended to. Her general unspoken message to everyone was, "This woman is my friend. Treat her like gold." There was a dialogue coach on hand just for me. All my scenes were with Jeanne and Jess, who cheerfully ran lines with me as long as I wanted, and the scenes themselves went surprisingly well considering that for the most part I didn't have a clue what I was doing. I didn't realize how stressed out I was by the newness of it and by wanting them not to regret that they'd hired me in the first place, and as soon as I delivered my last line and the director yelled, "Cut!" I burst into tears. Jeanne, who was sitting next to me on the couch, immediately put her arms around me, quietly said, "Let it out," and held onto me until I'd had the good cry I'd been saving up and pulled myself together. Thank you, Jeanne Cooper, for being exactly who you are and exactly who I needed at that very moment.

It speaks volumes about the worldwide popularity of that show that after who knows how many television appearances I'd made during all those decades, I never had more people call in or come rushing over out in public to excitedly say, "I saw you on *The Young and the Restless!*" And I'm enormously proud to announce that one of my three episodes now resides in the National Television Academy archives.

———

NOT LONG AFTERWARD, we got word that *The Montel Williams Show* was ending after seventeen years on the air. The news sent

Montel and me down so many nostalgic paths together, on screen and off, that we still reminisce about them, in between all the new directions our lives are taking. In the years we've known each other, we've gone through divorces, remarriages, issues with our children, soaring heights and crushing lows, and dealt with them side by side, each other's most loyal, outspoken advocate. I could devote an entire book just to him (I just pictured him reading that comment and breaking out in a cold sweat), from his stunning and intensely private generosity to the fact that he's the only man I know who'd respond to being diagnosed with MS by taking up snowboarding.

Our onstage memories are countless, but to share just a handful:

Montel and I had an ongoing competition that he couldn't resist reigniting every time he spotted a visibly pregnant woman in the audience. I believed I could predict psychically whether the baby was a boy or a girl. He believed he had a gift for being able to tell more accurately by touching the woman's stomach and checking out how high or low she was carrying it. We never did do follow-ups to find out which of us won that contest, but since this is my book, I'll say I did.

Montel always took great delight in watching my hair stand on end when anyone mentioned either wanting to meet or already having met his or her *soul mate*. I'll say it for the billionth time, bearing in mind that I used up at least half a billion of those times on Montel's show: please don't set yourself up for the inevitable disappointment of searching for or thinking you've found your soul mate! Your soul mate is the "identical twin" spirit who was created at the same time you were. The two of you are very close when you're on the Other Side together, but you're not joined at the hip, and you each have your own spiritual journey to take at your own pace in your own way. The chances of the two of you choosing to incarnate at exactly the same time and chart yourselves into each other's lives are virtually nonexistent. It's extremely likely that the soul mate you might be searching for so eagerly, and with so many "false alarms" along the way, is at Home right now waiting to hear all about your trip to earth, so you're looking for someone who's not even here. In the meantime, how liberating when you give up the hyper-romanticized idea of finding your soul mate: if and when someone you become intensely involved with disappoints you, mistreats you, or doesn't live up to those impossible soul mate expectations, you won't subject yourself to the huge letdown of believing you've been disappointed by that one person you thought you were destined to spend your lifetime with.

I gave Montel no end of nagging about maybe doing follow-ups or some kind of validation to things I said on the air. As I pointed out to him, without validation, I could just be sitting there making everything up as I went along for all anyone knew. On-air valida-tions never did become the general rule I was hoping for, but there was one case for which I'll always be grateful to his staff. It was a ghost story from a family in the audience who'd been seeing "strangers" in and around their house for several years. There was a man in work clothes who was always doing yard work and a small elderly woman in a simple long dark dress and an Amish-looking cap. These strangers would appear and disappear at random, and while they never seemed threatening, they were unnerving to the family who found themselves living with them. I assured them that these strangers were harmless; they were a man named Henry Beard and his mother, doing their usual chores around the house without a clue that they'd been dead for decades. Later in the show Montel's producer surprised me on camera by announcing that the staff had been hard at work making phone calls and checking the Internet, and they'd confirmed that the land on which the family was living was owned in the early 1900s by a family named Beard. This prompted an exchange between me and Montel that happened too many times to count over all those years:

MONTEL: How did you know that?
ME: I'm psychic.

And speaking of "too many times to count," Montel and I were asked over and over and over again, separately and together, if we sprinkled "ringers" throughout the audience when I was on to guarantee accuracy on my part. Sometimes I would meet guests before the show, and we would always make sure to clarify that on the air. But I've never used a ringer in my life, nor has Montel, and we always marveled that anyone would even suspect such a thing, for one simple reason: do you realize how many people over my more than fifteen years on the air with Montel would have to have kept their mouths shut in order for us to pull off a cheesy, unacceptable stunt like planting prearranged "coconspirators" in the audience? In this Internet world of instant news and no secrets that won't be unearthed sooner or later, no matter how personal, it wouldn't and couldn't happen.

One of the murder cases from Montel's show that touched me the most came from a wonderful couple in the audience I'll call Joe and Grace. Their beautiful eighteen-year-old daughter Cynthia (not really) had been shot to death in a parking lot while backing out of her parking space to head home from extra work on a music video. A security guard reported hearing gunshots and then discovering Cynthia behind the wheel, her car running and rolling backward, the driver's door open.

There were no fingerprints. There was no DNA. The murder weapon was nowhere to be found. There were no signs of robbery or sexual assault. And when I met Joe and Grace, the investigation was moving slowly due to the lack of evidence. Again, I was never involved in the investigation, but I was able to tell Joe and Grace that the man police should focus on would be particularly conspicuous because of his uniform—not that the uniform was flashy, but it was significant, probably with a blue shirt like that worn by a security guard. In fact, the security guard who first discovered Cynthia's body should be looked at very closely.

It took five years and an enormous amount of tenacity from law enforcement and from Joe and Grace, but ultimately that same security guard was arrested and charged with first-degree murder. After two hung juries resulting in mistrials, and a change of venue, the security guard in question was convicted of second-degree murder on December 18, 2009. To Joe and Grace: it was a longer wait for justice than anyone should have to endure, you've fought hard and with the greatest grace and integrity, and I'm so happy for you that you finally saw the justice you and Cynthia deserve. You're truly remarkable people, and you have my deepest admiration.

Nor have Montel and I ever forgotten the most chilling, peculiar good news/bad news validation of a suspect's guilt I've ever experienced in all my decades of work with law enforcement. Distraught parents I'll call George and Lynn were in the audience, hoping for answers in the murder of their young, beautiful daughter not really named Vanessa. The investigation in their small southern town seemed to be going nowhere, with several "persons of interest" but not enough evidence to narrow things down to any solid suspect. There was a volatile group of friends involved, with jealousy and rivalries and a lot of partying thrown in, and George and Lynn were desperate to know if I could come up with the name of anyone the police should be looking at more closely.

Montel's production staff had developed a policy years and years earlier of muting my voice when I was giving names or any other specific details that had to do with active criminal investigations, to protect the show and me from any legal liabilities. It wasn't an issue for me—I would say whatever I had to say, and it was up to the directors and the editors to worry about the legalities.

So when George and Lynn asked me for the name of Vanessa's killer, and that name psychically came to me loud and clear, I said it. "The police need to take a much closer look at someone your daughter knew named David."

They were stunned—they knew exactly who David was, and while they hadn't thought of him as a possible suspect before, something about my suggestion made horrible sense to them. They promised to share this bit of information along to the local police the minute they got home.

The show aired three weeks later. The editors had muted me so that I never audibly said the name "David." But the camera was on me at the time, and even the most amateur lipreader could very easily see that "David" was what I came up with.

A few hours after that episode was televised, the David in question committed suicide.

A subsequent investigation led to confirmation of David's guilt, and the murder was solved. It was a bittersweet, joyless validation. Vanessa's parents were relieved to know the identity of their daughter's killer, of course, but they were as heartbroken on behalf of David's parents as Montel and I were, and never again was I shown on camera saying the name of a potential suspect.

Then there was one of my last *Montel Williams Show* appearances, in which he treated me to a video retrospective of what I believe he called my "cavalcade of hairstyles" through the course of the series. Don't get me wrong, I was as amused as everyone else at my metamorphosis since the early 1990s, and in some cases I don't think I would have recognized myself on the street. But all things considered, it didn't really leave me a lot of options if I'd decided to do the same to him. Forget the hair, the man hasn't aged a day since we first introduced ourselves that morning on the *Queen Mary* twenty years ago.

We both loved every minute of *The Montel Williams Show*, and we miss it. But mark my words, you haven't seen the last of us, separately and together. That's a promise.

One late afternoon in October of 2007 Lindsay and I were sitting at Junior's, our favorite deli in Los Angeles, eating what we've come to think of as their "eternal chef's salad"—not only is it huge to begin with, but you can work on it for an hour and it still looks exactly like it did when the waitress brought it. (Our theory is that someone sits under the table shoving up lettuce through a hole in the bottom of the bowl.)

As we ate, and ate, and ate, we laughed a lot and cried a little at the countless changes in our lives in the nine years we'd known each other, and we spent a lot of time marveling over how blessed we both were. Our lives were filled with dogs (I had five, she had four), families, friends and careers we loved, not one bit of which we took for granted or would have changed for anything in the world.

"And I'll tell you another thing," I remember saying as if it were yesterday. "I'm through with relationships. Been there, done that to death. I have everything I want and need, and there's not a chance in hell I'm going to complicate my life by falling in love ever again. I know the old adage 'Never say never,' but I can say it and mean it— *never*! *That* you can count on."

Lindsay, who's been around the block a few times herself, raised her iced-tea glass to mine and we toasted our independent, self-sufficient, relationship-free happiness.

And then, three months later, I walked into a jewelry store in Campbell, California, and heard myself asking about that attractive man behind the counter.

What do you know, they're right after all: Never say "never."

So here I sit in 2010, looking back and looking forward.

Paul is now happily married to his second wife Heather.

Chris and Gina are divorced and still good friends. Chris's career as a psychic is brilliantly successful, and he's hard at work on a new book.

Mary is regularly traveling with me when I tour, and we're enjoying every minute of our time together.

My grandchildren are thriving and continue to be the joys of my life. By the time you read this, Angelia will have graduated from high school. She's chosen to explore her own path rather than follow in her Bagdah's and father's footsteps, and we couldn't be more proud of her.

Dal is in great hands at an assisted living facility, where he's found a lovely girlfriend.

———————

AS FOR ME, I'm a very happily married woman. So *this* is what that looks like. Michael is a smart, talented, kind, truly alive man. He has his own identity and his own career, earns his own living, treats me beautifully, adores my children and grandchildren (and his own), and—I hope you're sitting down—doesn't have the slightest interest in handling my finances. In fact, I've added a business manager and a forensic accounting firm to my team to make long overdue sense of that aspect of my past and my future. I have a beautiful, brilliant literary agent named Jennifer DeChiara. She introduced me to my new publisher, HarperOne, who've made me feel valued and very much at home from the moment we met.

I wake up every morning looking forward to the day ahead.

If it can happen for me, God knows it can happen for you. And I do mean *God knows*. You and He planned this lifetime together, don't forget, and He, your Spirit Guide, your Angels, your totem, and all your loved ones on the Other Side are with you every minute, watching over you and loving you and seeing to it that no matter what happens or how overwhelming things sometimes seem, you'll never go through them alone. It's another promise from your Creator that you can count on, now and eternally.

———————

WITH ALL MY heart, I thank you, I love you, and I wish you the joy that comes from devoting your life to the one simple, unconditional purpose we're all here to satisfy:

> *Do good,*
> *love God,*
> *then shut up and go Home.*

AFTERWORD

We never fully understand the purpose and course of our charts until we're Home again, but writing this book has helped mine make so much more sense to me than ever before. (Of course, added credit for clarity goes to Francine and her favorite rhetorical question, "What have you learned when times were good?")

Looking back on my life as a progression of pre-planned stepping stones rather than a random series of stupid decisions is what allows me to proudly call myself a survivor, not a victim—never a victim—because I am responsible for every choice I made and how I handled those choices. If you have trouble appreciating your own chart in terms of hurdles that can be transformed into stepping stones if you handle them properly and learn from them in the long run, feel free to use mine as an example:

If I hadn't had Grandma Ada, I might have hidden in fear from my gifts instead of living a full, blessed life devoting those gifts to God.

If I hadn't had a father who believed in me, sometimes enough for both of us, I might have let self-doubt confine me to only a fraction of what I have to offer.

If I hadn't had a mother with whom I shared a mutual dislike, I might have been drawn into her darkness rather than repelled by it.

If I hadn't married Gary I wouldn't have Paul and Chris and Angelia and Willy and Jeffrey, and I can't imagine the emptiness of my life without them. I wouldn't have moved to California, where my purpose was waiting. And I might not have learned that when it comes to the safety and well-being of my children, there's no such thing as hesitation or compromise.

If I hadn't had the perfectly timed blessing of Bob Williams' inspiration, followed by my marriage to Dal, I might never have had the courage and support to form the Nirvana Foundation and expand the horizons of my gifts far beyond anything I'd imagined.

If I hadn't had Larry's tireless efforts on my behalf when my marriage to Dal ended so hideously, that whole ugly public and personal disaster might have destroyed me beyond my ability to recover.

If Larry hadn't done me the favor of leaving exactly when and how he left, I might never have had the truly enlightening experience of learning to treasure my own company, my independence, and the lesson learned that we really are on this earth to overcome negativity, not to wallow in it, marry it, or let our self-worth be compromised by it.

If it hadn't been for all of that and all the rest, I wouldn't have found the love of my life, Michael, and I might never have earned the happiness, peace, and purpose that fill my days enough to allow me to write this book and understand with a spirit wiser than when I got here the old adage from Confucius, "Our greatest glory is not in never falling but in rising every time we fall."

ACKNOWLEDGMENTS

Our eternal love and gratitude to our spectacular agent, Jennifer DeChiara, and to Catherine Hickland, who guided us to her. Jennifer, this book would never have become a reality without you.

Our countless thanks to Nancy Hancock and everyone at Harper-One for opening your arms to us and making us feel so welcome and so much at home.

To Linda Rossi—never think we don't know and appreciate how hard you work on every project, including this one.

And to attorney Tom Krucker, for his constant help along the way, not the least of which included his gentle promise, "If you don't let me review those contracts before you sign them, I'll kill you."

Sylvia